Copy 1

This Life I've Led

my autobiography

by

Babe Didrikson Zaharias

as told to

Harry Paxton

A. S. BARNES AND COMPANY

New York

In memory of
my mother and father,
and to my husband, George,
without whom
there never would have been
a life to lead.

Preface

You might suppose offhand that Babe Didrikson Zaharias is too well known to require any introduction. Actually this isn't the case. To be sure, even people who never look at the sports pages can identify her as a superwoman athlete. And everybody is sympathetically aware of her valiant struggle against cancer. But only a comparative few have been in a position to know that she is also something out of the ordinary as a person.

Hundreds of newspaper reporters, among others, have made this pleasant discovery at different places around the country during the past two decades. The Babe would come to their town for some tournament or personal appearance. They would be assigned to interview her. They would go out expecting, as often as not, to meet a hard-shelled muscle woman. They would find instead one of the most exuberantly warm and openhearted human beings ever to turn up on the sports beat.

Yet their stories about the Babe, being necessarily limited in scope and space, seldom have conveyed the full flavor and dimensions of her personality. A news reporter must, as a rule, concentrate on some one angle. He sifts out the most striking and pertinent "quotes." In the Babe's case, this sort of highlighting is inadequate to give the picture. The truth is that Babe Didrikson Zaharias is more than just a sports figure. And her life has been much more than just a sports story.

This writer has done many biographical pieces about prominent athletes, and helped a number of others to tell their own stories. Always the effort is to get beneath the surface and bring ones subject to life. Most of the time it is an effort, calling for intensive digging not only with the man himself, but also with people close to him. Some great athletes are too shy and introverted to talk much about themselves. Some are too inarticulate. A few just don't have much to say; they are pretty commonplace individuals when considered apart from their sports specialties.

There are others who do respond freely and fully to searching questions. A handful, such as Leo Durocher, can be real spellbinders. But the writer never has worked with anyone in sports who "gave" so unreservedly as the Babe. At each slight prod she would be off and running, volunteering her every thought and emotion about the topic up for discussion.

When preparation of this autobiography began, Babe said, "If I'm going to tell the story of my life, the thing for me to do is relive it." And she did. For instance, when you come to the chapter relating how she was sent to Chicago as a one-girl track team to try and win the national women's championship singlehanded, you will read this passage: "It came time to announce my 'team.' I spurted out there all alone, waving my arms, and you never heard such a roar. It brought out goose bumps all over me. I can feel them now, just thinking about it."

Well, Babe was sitting in her Florida home when she

viii

said these words, and wearing her usual around-the-house attire of shorts and blouse. She paused for a moment and looked down at herself. Sure enough, she had been "reliving" that moment so completely that her bare arms and legs were covered with gooseflesh.

There was no subject on which the Babe said, "I'd rather not get into that," or, "Let's leave that out." She never stopped to calculate her words so as to put the best possible construction on potentially controversial matters. On all phases of her life, the details flowed out with the characteristic spontaneity of this woman who doesn't try to fool anybody—including herself.

In line with this, a short explanation is in order on how this book came into being. For years people had been telling Babe Zaharias, "You should write your memoirs. You've had such an unusual life." And she had kept answering, "I'll never have the time for it." She probably never would have had the time to do a thoroughgoing job if it had been necessary for her to put the whole thing in manuscript form herself. What made this book possible was that modern improvement on the old-fashioned ghost writer—the tape recorder.

Most public figures with interesting and significant lives to talk about do need some specialized assistance in preparing their stories for publication. Unfortunately, the subject's words and thoughts often are diluted considerably in transmission through a collaborator. This is particularly regrettable when the subject is a person of genuine individuality, such as Babe Didrikson Zaharias.

So when her good friend and business agent, Fred Corcoran, flashed the word last winter, "Babe's ready to tell her story now," it was promptly decided that she should tell it in the presence of a tape recorder. As she re-created her life stage by stage—reminiscing out loud for hours at a time, day after day—the machine was there to capture precisely all her words and opinions and attitudes. Nothing was left to the fallible memory and notebook of the collaborator. In assembling it all on paper, he worked with pure ore.

So this is the Babe's own story, told in her own natural, informal—and vivid—style of expressing herself. It is as revealing as utter candor can make it, although she indulges in no hand-wringing self-analysis. That wouldn't be the Babe. She isn't the type for repressions and neuroses. She doesn't lock up her troubles inside herself. Her problems always are out in the open. She doesn't brood about them. She acts on them.

If there is anything you don't understand about the Babe when you have finished this book, it won't be because she tried to hold things back. She doesn't draw many conclusions about herself, but the various facets of her character are implicit in her personal testimony.

For example, take the big question: What made her such a phenomenal athlete? Was she born that way? You will see from the evidence that although she was a "natural" with great innate ability, it by no means followed automatically that she should become the champ. Read about how she kept drilling for her first important golf tournament until there was "tape all over my hands, and blood all over the tape."

They say in sports that "the best athlete is the hungry athlete." You will find that this applies to the Babe in the sense that she knew financial insecurity as a child. However, she had security in the broader sense that the child psychologists talk about—she grew up in an exceptionally close-knit and affectionate household. This is clear from Babe's fond reminiscences about her Norwegian-born Momma and Poppa, and her six brothers and sisters. It has been reflected throughout her life in her cheerful, friendly outlook on the world and everybody in it.

You will realize also that some of her remarks which sound boastful when taken out of context actually are plain statements of the truth as she sees it. Frank Graham, the distinguished New York sports columnist, has remarked that in this respect Babe reminds him of baseball's Roger Hornsby—a quite different personality in other ways. Each has an outspoken honesty that is uninhibited either by vainglory or false modesty. Each lays it right on the line, without striving for any calculated effect.

The Babe doesn't pretend to be anything more than what she is. Nor does she pretend to be anything less. When she speaks of her skills, she does so without preening herself or getting belligerently insistent. She is relaxed about it. Her tone is matter-of-fact.

Most of the work on this book was done during a period in the spring of 1955 when the Babe was taking what she regarded as a rest. She had been feeling a bit fatigued, and had decided to take several weeks off from the golf-tournament circuit. This would be a good time for the autobiography, she thought, and also for the Zahariases to move into their brand-new Tampa home, on which final touches still were being made.

When she wasn't pouring her life story into the tape recorder, she was busy superintending—and often working with—assorted electricians and other installation men. Some rest cure! At that, it was a comparative breathing spell for this hyperactive gal who always has lived and worked at a furious morning-to-night pace.

In the course of spending many days with the Zahariases, the collaborator could see for himself the validity of many of the things the Babe was bringing out in her memoirs. There was the easy oneness that existed between the Babe and her husband George. There was the devoted friendship of her young golfing protégé, Betty Dodd, who was in there helping at every step as the Babe and George settled into their new house.

One of the notable features of this book is the Babe's lack of animosity toward the occasional persons and organizations whose actions have impeded her progress. She seldom expresses even mild resentment, and in no case does she indicate any lasting feeling of ill will. She's the same way in private conversation. She doesn't go in for backbiting and running people down. Malice and spite are not part of her make-up.

Her manner is the same with anyone she meets, from laborers to Presidents. She never was overawed by celebrities, even before she became one herself. She doesn't try to overawe anyone else.

Enough of stating things that the reader will be able to see for himself. The purpose of this preface is not to try to summarize the book. On the pages that follow, the Babe will reveal herself much more clearly and interestingly than any outsider could hope to do.

She's a person worth knowing. Can you think of any other athlete in history, man or woman, who has been supreme in so many different fields? The Babe has been tops in every sport she took up—an All-American in basketball, a world-record breaker in track and field, a consistent winner of all the major golf championships open to women.

Perhaps her most impressive golfing triumphs—fully as amazing as those achieved by Ben Hogan after his near-fatal automobile smashup—were the titles she came back to win after undergoing major cancer surgery in 1953. Many persons who have this same operation resign themselves to being semi-invalids the rest of their lives.

It is probable that the sobering effect of her cancer ordeal, combined with the evidence that her comeback had been inspirational to other sufferers, hastened the Babe's decision last winter to delay no longer on doing her autobiography. She still was only forty when she began these memoirs, but she already had been established for a quarter of a century in the world of big-time sports.

There was one unhappy new note just as this book was being completed in the summer of 1955. The Babe had met and licked cancer once. Now the doctors found that she was in for a return match. Their X rays showed a fresh trace of cancer.

This news did not demoralize her, any more than other tough challenges have. The Babe always has been the happy-warrior type—determined but not bitter. She is a realistic competitor who never underrates an opponent—and never doubts that she has what it takes to come out on top. It was in this spirit that she faced up to the latest big battle of her demanding life.

—Harry T. Paxton

This Life I've Led

CHAPTER 1

You never saw anybody more excited than I was that night at the railroad station in Beaumont, Texas, back in February 1930. Here I was, just a little old high-school girl, wanting to be a big athlete. And now I was getting a chance to go with an insurance company in Dallas and play on their basketball team in the women's national championships.

It was an overnight sleeper trip to Dallas, about 275 miles from Beaumont. To me, that was like going to Europe. I'd never been more than a few miles away from home in my life. I'd hardly ever been so dressed up, either. I was wearing the blue silk dress with box pleats that I'd made in school,

3

and won a prize with at the Texas State Fair. I had on my patent leather shoes, and socks, and the little hat I'd got for graduation exercises at junior high school. I was carrying a black patent leather purse. It had my entire fortune in it—the $3.49 change from the money they'd given me to buy the railroad tickets.

My dad was traveling with me. I took the upper berth and Poppa took the lower. He propped himself up with his newspaper and started puffing away on his big black pipe, the way he always did at home. For a while there they thought that Pullman car was on fire.

In Dallas the next morning Col. M. J. McCombs, the man who was in charge of the basketball team, met us at the station with the big yellow Cadillac he used for driving the girls around to games. He had a redcap take our bags and put them in the car, and then tipped him a quarter.

I said to Poppa, "Look at that! He gets a quarter just for carrying those bags out. Man, I'd like to get me a job like that!"

I'll bet I've traveled a couple of million miles since then, competing all around the United States and in other parts of the world, but that first trip was the start of everything. Even then I had other ideas besides playing basketball. I wanted to be in the Olympic Games, and after that I wanted to be a golf star. One thing sort of led to another. I got to be an Olympic champion, and win all the most important women's golf tournaments, and do a lot of other things.

It didn't all go along as smooth as that sounds. I wanted to spend my life in sports, but I had to make money too, and that isn't so easy for a woman athlete. There were times when I could have used that redcap's quarters. Once I got so hard up I almost agreed to a stunt where they'd have me running a race against a horse. But I didn't do it. I knew that wasn't really the right kind of performance for a girl to be putting on.

Those money worries I used to have were nothing like the jolt that hit me in April of 1953. The doctors found I had a cancer in the lower intestine. They told me I needed an operation called a colostomy, and explained what it was. It changes your anatomy around so much that you wonder whether you'll ever be able to live your normal life again. That was all I could think of when I first got the bad news.

Finally I took hold of myself. I said, "Babe, here you're worrying about whether you can play in golf tournaments, you're worrying about whether you can give exhibitions, you're worrying about whether you can go to banquets. You'd better start realizing that you'll be doing good if you get out of this thing alive."

All my life I've been competing—and competing to win. I came to realize that in its way, this cancer was the toughest competition I'd faced yet. I made up my mind that I was going to lick it all the way. I not only wasn't going to let it kill me, I wasn't even going to let it put me on the shelf. I was determined to come back and win golf championships just the same as before.

I lived through the cancer, and I've been living with it since. I want to say more about that later, because I believe the cancer problem should be out in the open. The more the public knows about it the better.

I won't ever forget the first golf tournament I played in after my cancer operation. It was the 1953 Tam o' Shanter "All-American Championship" in Niles, Illinois, and I entered it about three and a half months after being under the knife.

I had a bad round the first day—an eighty-two. The second day it was worse—an eighty-five. It seemed like I couldn't do anything right. The third day started off the same. I was beginning to think it was true what so many people had said, that I'd never be able to play championship golf again.

I three-putted the fourth green. On the fifth hole I messed up an easy little chip shot, and then took another three putts. I walked on to the sixth tee, and sat down on my seat cane. And then—I couldn't stop myself—I put my face in my hands and just bawled.

My friend Betty Dodd, the young golfer, was paired with me that day, and also Beverly Hanson. That big, wonderful guy I'm married to, George Zaharias, was walking around the course with us. Wait'll I get to tell you how I first met up with him! Anyway, George and Betty both said I should pick up and go back to the clubhouse if I didn't feel like playing any more that afternoon. They said everybody would understand and think it was perfectly all right.

I told them, "I don't pick up the ball!" I went on and played out the round, and my game began coming back. I shot the last nine holes in thirty-four, two under men's par. By the next year, 1954, I was winning tournaments again, including the biggest one, the National Women's Open. That was the third Women's Open I'd won out of the five I've played in.

I really pointed for that 1954 Open, and I took it by twelve strokes. You have to get yourself all fired up to win these tournaments. It's even harder to stay at the top in sports than it is to get there.

It took me longer than I figured it would to get to the top in golf. The thing was that in the early years, I couldn't stick with golf all the time, the way you have to do if you're going to develop your game. I had a living to make, and a family I wanted to help. I wanted to do things for Momma and Poppa. They'd done so much for us seven Didrikson kids.

I had a wonderful childhood. That must prove that it doesn't take money to be happy, because the Didriksons sure weren't rich. My father and mother had to work and scrimp and save like anything just to be able to feed and clothe us all. Poppa's trade there in Beaumont was furniture refinishing. He did fine cabinet work, and most of the time he was making around $200 a month. That was pretty good money in those days, but with seven kids to support, he generally didn't have any dimes or quarters to hand out to us for picture shows and all that.

So Poppa said, "Well, I'll build good bodies for them." He set up a regular gymnasium in the back yard. He put up bars for jumping and all that. In the garage he had this weightlifting device. It was an old broomstick with a flatiron at each end. He put it there for the boys, so they could strengthen their muscles, but my sister Lillie and I would get in there and work out with it too.

The last four of us were pretty close together in age— Louis and Lillie, who were twins; little brother Arthur, and me. Lillie and I always barged right into all the neighborhood games along with Louis and Arthur. So did a girl friend of ours named Christine McCandless. We played baseball and football with the boys and everything.

I know the boys there on Doucette Street in Beaumont hated to see us girls show up when they were playing football.

That meant they'd have to stop tackling and switch to touch tag. My mother always said to my brothers, "Don't tackle the girls." My brothers were in the games, of course, so they knew that if there was any tackling, and Momma heard about it, they'd catch it when they got home.

We'd play baseball in our back yard, and sometimes the ball would go into the rose bushes. Poor Momma nearly died, because she really loved her roses. I'm the same way about roses myself. Momma kept telling us to keep that baseball out of her flower beds. Then one day we persuaded her to get in the game herself. She hit a ball right into the rose bushes. We never heard any more complaints from her about our ballplaying after that.

My mother and father were both from Norway. They were already married and had three children when they came to this country. My dad was Ole Didrikson—that's pronounced Oh-lee. I believe his own father was a cabinet maker in Oslo, but Poppa spent the first part of his life going to sea. He went around Cape Horn on sailing vessels something like seventeen times.

What a bang we used to get out of his stories about his experiences! We'd huddle around him and listen like mad. I'm not sure to this day whether he was kidding some of the time or not. He'd tell us about leaving home and making his first voyage at the age of nine. He'd describe one trip where they got stranded on an island, and kept themselves alive by eating monkeys and things. Then he'd tell about a voyage around Cape Horn where his ship broke up in a storm and he clung to a mast rope by one hand for hours, holding another guy up with his other hand. It could all be true. Things like that happened to those old seafarers.

8

Poppa could do wonderful things with tools. I still have a beautiful ship model in a bottle that he made in Liverpool, England, in 1905. He'd get a little ship all made, with the masts lying down, and slide the ship into the bottle. Then he'd pull a string that brought the masts up taut, and fasten it all securely with a special knot.

Poppa let Momma handle the money in our house. She was a good manager. I never liked to go downtown and get new shoes with Momma, because she'd buy me a cheap pair. But when I went with Poppa, why, he'd get me those six-dollar shoes.

If Poppa happened to have a little extra change, and us four youngest ones asked for money to go to a picture show or something, he'd make us wrestle him for it. We'd all jump on Poppa and finally get him down, and he'd give us enough for the movies and popcorn too.

Momma's maiden name was Hannah Marie Olson. She was the daughter of a shoemaker in Bergen, Norway. She was a little shorter than I am, about five feet four. You could tell by the way she handled herself that she was a natural athlete. When I was grown up, I once got her to try swinging a golf club. She had the prettiest swing you ever saw for someone who'd never done it before.

When I got to be a sports champion, Poppa would kid around and say, "Well, she must get it from me." But I think that as far as athletics are concerned, I probably took after my mother. I understand she was considered the finest woman ice skater and skier around her part of Norway. When she was little, her dad couldn't afford to buy her skis, so he made her a pair out of barrel staves. She'd get on them and go like the wind from where she lived down into the city.

Skiing is one sport I never got to try myself until 1948, when I was appearing in the Sportsmen's Show in Boston. I was connected with a shoe company near there—the Adams Company, of Amherst, New Hampshire, which was making a line of Babe Zaharias golf shoes. I was staying with Mr. Adams' sister. She had three children who were very good skiers, and she was a skier herself.

One day we went out to teach me skiing. A Boston sportswriter who watched us wrote that I was catching on pretty fast. Naturally I didn't try the big hills or anything like that. And I took my tumbles. Once I was coming down the first hill, which was about a hundred yards or so. I'd have run right into a barbwire fence if I hadn't jumped. They told me it was the prettiest jump they ever saw—for not landing on two feet.

Momma's own skiing ended when she came to Texas, of course. The way that happened was this. After she and Poppa were married and raising a family in Oslo, one of his voyages was on an oil tanker that went to Port Arthur in Texas. He really liked it down there on the Gulf of Mexico. When he got back to Oslo, he told Momma that as soon as he could get enough money together, he was going to bring them all to Port Arthur to live.

Momma got excited about the idea too. Finally they saved enough money to come over. They landed in Port Arthur with their three kids, Dora and Esther Nancy and young Ole. One of the first things that caught Momma's eye, right as she stepped off the pier, was a beautiful potato bowl in a store window. It was the old-fashioned kind with a lid on it and an opening for the ladle. Poppa bought Momma that potato bowl, and I have it in my own house today. It's cracked and all, but I wouldn't part with it for anything.

The Didriksons settled right down in Port Arthur. Poppa gave up the sea and went into furniture refinishing, following his father's old trade. Momma and Poppa lived in different houses in Port Arthur. They rented for a while, and then Poppa built a two-story house that looked like a ship. Every house that we lived in had to have a flagpole. America was Poppa's country now, and he always wanted the flag out on the Fourth of July and Armistice Day and all the other holidays.

In Port Arthur the family increased. First there were the twins, Louis and Lillie. Then I arrived on June 26, 1914—Mildred Ella Didrikson. Finally there was Arthur. He was "Bubba," for little brother. I was "Baby." They were still calling me "Baby" when I was in school, until Momma said I was getting too old for a nickname like that. Then they switched to my regular name, Mildred, or Millie. The "Babe" came later, when I began hitting home runs in ball games. Babe Ruth was the big hero then, and the kids said, "She's a regular Babe Ruth. We'll call her Babe."

We picked up and moved seventeen miles from Port Arthur to Beaumont when I was about three and a half. The thing I remember best from the Port Arthur days is that we had a next-door neighbor who was the fireman, and kept the fire truck in his back yard. He also had a bull which he kept in a vacant lot. I must have teased that bull, because it would get loose and chase me. I'd run and jump up on the fire truck where the bull couldn't get at me. I'd stay there until someone took the bull away and lifted me down.

In Beaumont Poppa bought a little two-bedroom house on Doucette Street. I think he paid something like $2500 for it back there around 1918. It was two bedrooms, kitchen, dining room, living room. That wasn't really big enough for a family the size of ours, and Poppa kept adding onto it until it became the biggest house on the block.

He started off by building a big enclosed porch all the way around the back. I'd say it was about forty feet by twenty-five or thirty feet. He put beds out there for the boys, so the girls could have one of the bedrooms. But that still meant that four of us were sleeping in the one room. So he finally partitioned the porch and put the girls in one half and the boys in the other. It was real fresh-air sleeping. That porch had twenty-eight windows in it.

When I was recovering from my cancer operation in the hospital in Beaumont in 1953, and got well enough to be taken for automobile rides by my husband George and Betty Dodd, I had them drive me down to Doucette Street. Betty found a spot in the pavement where I'd drawn "M.E.D.-A.S.D."— the initials of myself and my brother Arthur. I'd drawn the date too. I think it was 1926.

I often visit the old block when I'm in Beaumont. I've gone through the house we lived in. The people who own it now have made a lot of changes, of course, but it still looks mighty familiar.

The whole neighborhood still looks familiar, although it's changed a lot too. Mamaschella's store isn't there anymore. That was a grocery run by this Italian family. One of the things we used to love was roller skating, and the best place for it was the pavement outside Mamaschella's. We'd have regular skating parties there—the Mamaschella kids and all the rest of us. You'd whip along where the bananas were hanging and grab one as you went by. The Mamaschellas never could figure out why their bananas kept disappearing so fast.

When I was a little kid I'd sometimes do odd jobs in the store. I'd measure out things like potatoes and rice and sugar and flour. I'd weigh them and put them up in bags— one pound, five pounds, ten pounds or whatever was wanted. They'd pay me off in candy and stuff like that which I generally had no pennies to buy.

Right across the street from us lived this woman who had been a circus performer. Her name was Aunt Minnie. She did an aerial act where she'd hang by her teeth at the top of the tent, and they'd spin her around. And she did this 250-foot slide, still holding by the teeth, and they caught her down below. She was the aunt of our friend Christine McCandless.

When the circus came to town Aunt Minnie would take the whole bunch of us and show us everything. Then we'd come back home and try to do the acrobatics ourselves. Anything athletic I always seemed to enjoy. We'd put on union suits, like circus tights. I remember one year we hung a whole series of trapezes in a Chinaberry tree Momma had planted in our back yard. We had one swing after another. We killed that tree, and it's a wonder we didn't kill ourselves, because we fell on our heads and everything.

I've never had a broken arm or leg or any other bad injury in my whole life. I don't know how I escaped it, when I think of some of the stunts we pulled as kids. We'd catch a ride on a horse and wagon out to the old saw mill to pick blackberries for Momma to can. We'd pick the berries real

13

fast, and then play all day long in the sawdust pile. It was as big as a house. We'd get to the top and then practically throw ourselves down it.

Once they were building a new house in the neighborhood, and we were playing follow-the-leader there. They almost always had me be the leader. Just the framework of the house was up—the studs and the flat rafters. I led the kids in climbing all over there. There was a sand pile alongside the house. I jumped into it from the top of the house. There was a sliver of wood in the sand pile, and it went right into the side of my leg. I still have the scar—it's the shape of a golf driver.

But after I had that taken care of, I was back out there leading them the next day. I started up to the top of the house again, and missed my step, and came down on my side with a terrible thump. My whole leg was skinned and bruised. I'd have got a whipping for sure after messing myself up a second time like that, if they hadn't found when I got home that I had three cracked ribs.

We lived like the average American family of twenty-five and thirty years ago. Every Saturday night you took your main bath of the week to clean the outside of your body, and then every other Sunday you had to take a dose of castor oil to clean out the inside. Two of us got the castor oil on one Sunday, and the other two the next. The oldest three were let off. Those that didn't get the castor oil had to go to Sunday school. We didn't like that either—we'd rather have spent the whole day playing.

A bottle of castor oil went pretty fast, with the great big tablespoon Poppa used for dishing it out. I'm telling you, he really had to go look for us when he came around with that

14

bottle! We'd be hiding behind chairs or under a bed or something. But he'd find us wherever we were, and make us swallow it down. After the castor oil, we each got half an orange. Then Poppa would have us drink some hot black coffee. He made sure we got cleaned out, all right.

Much as I hated castor oil, I remember that the first radio entertainer I liked, back when I was seven or eight years old, was a harmonica player who called himself Castor Oil Clarence. When they had crystal sets, one of my brothers made one. I used to lie in bed with the earphones on every Friday night and listen to that harmonica playing. It just fascinated me.

I wanted a harmonica myself, but my dad couldn't spare the money for one. So I took our lawn mower and went out and cut some neighbors' grass. The grass was so high that I had to use a sickle on it before I could mow it. And I earned enough money to get me a harmonica. I believe I paid about thirty-five cents for it. The same harmonica today would cost two dollars or more.

I'd lie in our hammock in the back yard and practice. "Home Sweet Home" was the first piece I learned to play, and then "Old Black Joe" and "Way Down Upon The Swanee River." I was going to get me a radio program like Castor Oil Clarence. I never did do that, but I got to where I could play pretty good.

At first I just practiced my harmonica in the hammock or on the back porch, but finally I'd go out on the front porch where the family could hear me. Our whole family was musical. My brothers played the drums. Two sisters played the piano, and the other played the violin. Poppa could play the violin too. Momma sang.

We had a family orchestra going there on the front porch at night after dinner. We put out some real Southern music. That's what Beaumont is—a real Southern town. Other kids would gather around in our front yard. And you could see the lights going off in houses all up and down the block as people got through with their dishes, and came out on their own porches to listen.

It was just a wonderful family life we had there. I don't mean that we didn't have our little spats, or that there were never any bad times for the Didriksons. There were times when things were plenty tough.

CHAPTER 2

The toughest period for the Didrikson family came when I was still a little kid. For several years there Poppa couldn't get work regularly. He had to go back to sea now and again when he couldn't find any jobs in Beaumont. And Momma took in washing.

All of us pitched in and helped her, so she wouldn't wear herself out. Little as I was, I'd wear my knuckles down scrubbing on that wash board. We'd wash the clothes and rinse them and hang them out, and then while that was drying we'd do another wash.

Momma had a friend in Port Arthur named Mrs. Hanson. She was Norwegian too. I remember her husband had a great big mustache. He was a chef on some big passenger liner. I think Mrs. Hanson was the only close friend my mother had. Momma was more interested in young kids than in people her own age. Every neighborhood she lived in, the kids were just crazy about her.

Anyway, during that tough period Mrs. Hanson would come up from Port Arthur for dinner several times a week and bring a big roast or something. Her husband was away most of the time, and making good money, and they had only one daughter of their own. Even when the husband was home, they'd visit us as much as three or four times a week, and they not only brought the food, Mr. Hanson would insist on fixing the meal himself.

Mrs. Hanson came to see Momma a lot both in good times and bad. They'd rest in Momma's bedroom while us kids were supposed to be doing the same on the porch. Poppa had put in a French door between the bedroom and the porch so Momma could keep an eye on us. She and Mrs. Hanson would be reading and gabbing. When they didn't want us to know what they were saying, they'd talk in Norwegian.

Mrs. Hanson loved to have me scratch her head. I'd do that by the hour for her, and she'd give me a quarter. I knew when she came to visit that I was going to get a quarter, and also that she would bring some coffee cake for all of us.

Except for that one bad spell, we always had plenty to eat, although it generally was on the plain side. Momma had to go in a lot for things like soup that were inexpensive, but filling and nourishing.

The meal that I think helped keep us all healthy and strong was a big, thick bowl of oatmeal every morning. My dad would get up about six o'clock and put the double boiler

18

on for the oatmeal. And he'd put the coffee on, and bring Momma her coffee in bed. She always got that, and I've been getting it all my grown-up life too.

Poppa would start the oatmeal cooking, and set out the bowls around the table. There were six bowls. The oldest child, Dora, wanted eggs instead. She was already working, and contributing six dollars a week for her room and board. When the oatmeal was ready, Poppa would dish it out in the bowls. He'd put butter in the middle and sugar on the top, and cover each bowl with a plate to keep it warm. By the time we got down it was all nice and melted. We were always hungry as bears. We'd gobble up the oatmeal, and a couple of slices of bread, and be all set to start the day.

Another dish we grew up on was the Norwegian meat balls that Momma made. She'd take ground meat and cracker crumbs, and mix it with chopped onions and chopped green peppers and things of that sort. She'd let the meat balls brown and simmer a long time, and serve them with onion gravy.

I make them myself today, except that now I add a lot of tomato paste and stuff to build up the flavor. And since I married George, whose family was Greek, I've learned to use a Greek herb called oregano. But Momma made her meat balls the plain way, which is very good.

There'd always be some left over the next day. When we got home from school, we'd slice up those meat balls and anything else that was around, and make ourselves sandwiches big enough to throw Dagwood for a loss.

Then there was *Jule kaka*, which is Norwegian for Yule cake, or Christmas cake. Momma would make twenty or thirty loaves of it at a time. It was the best stuff. One of my brother's wives bakes it now, almost like Momma used to. I've tried it a couple of times myself, but I haven't been able to hit it right. I'd start out with a great big pan of dough and come out with one little loaf.

Poppa loved fish balls. Every Friday on his way home from work he'd stop by the fish market and bring home a big red snapper or a cod or something. If he wasn't able to get to the market himself, he'd send one of us down for it. In those days you just bought a fish—it wasn't cleaned or anything. Poppa would scale it and clean it, and then I'd generally have to grind it up for the fish balls. Momma would mix in potatoes and things to stretch it.

If we happened to have a turkey or a chicken, it always seemed to be my turn to kill it. We'd hang it up and let it dry, and then put hot water on it and pick the feathers. When it got on the table I wouldn't be able to eat any. I couldn't stand to kill something like that and then eat it.

There were plenty of chores for all of us to do. When family washday came, each of the girls had certain things to iron. My job was to iron the boys' khaki shirts and pants. With three or four for each boy every week, that got kind of rough.

Momma was a good organizer. She'd divide up the work so that everything got done. And we didn't realize it then, but she was also teaching us. She was showing us that everyone has responsibilities in life. Everyone has jobs they must do.

At night we all had to shine our shoes. I wore mine to school, but I was barefoot the rest of the time, except on Sundays. We'd have that polish box out, and everybody would be trying to shine their shoes at once. And we had to take turns at shining Momma's shoes and Poppa's shoes.

20

There were those twenty-eight windows in the porch to be washed every Saturday, and the grocery shopping to be done. We'd go down to a store near the Magnolia Refinery. My mother would make out the list, and Lillie and I would go down there with this little wagon. We'd get it loaded way up. I remember that the bill for a week's shopping would come to sixteen or seventeen dollars, and I'd think, "My gosh, all that money for this!" Nowadays the same load of groceries would probably cost you fifty or sixty dollars.

Another job was scrubbing floors. Poppa put in linoleum floors because they'd be easier to clean than wooden ones. Momma always believed in scrubbing the floor on your hands and knees. And you had to wash the woodwork all the time, and get in the corners. She'd tell me, "Don't let that dirt in the corner laugh at you! Get it out!"

I'd have that big back porch to scrub, and I'd get out there with the bucket and the scrub brushes. I'd put soap suds all over it, and if Momma wasn't watching, I'd take a run and slide the length of the floor. It scares me to death to think about it now, because there were these metal strips which held the linoleum in place. Once I slit my knee wide open sliding around like that.

And I'd fasten scrub brushes to my feet, and skate around on the soap suds. Sometimes I'd be in a hurry to go out and play, and I'd skimp the job. Momma would see the marks on the floor where I hadn't rinsed it real good. She'd take me by the ear and lead me over to it and say, "Babe, look at that. Is that right?" And I'd say, "No, ma'am, that's not right. But I had to leave. The ball game was going to start." She'd say, "Well, you go do it now. And do it right."

My parents were sweetly strict. Once Momma made me a nice new dress. I went off to school in it, and then after school I played in it. I snagged it on something and tore it.

When I came home Momma was in the kitchen cooking supper. A couple of days before she'd had an accident getting off the streetcar. The door caught her foot—they closed it too fast—and she sprained her ankle. So Momma was in the kitchen, trying to hobble around on this great big swollen ankle. And here I came in all dirty, and with a big tear in my brand new dress.

She just blew up. She started after me, trying to run on that ankle. I said, "Momma, don't run. I'll wait for you." She came up to me, and was going to spank me. Then she looked at me and began to laugh. She said, "I can't whip you."

We all just loved Momma, and Poppa too. We were forever hugging them and all that. I'd go lie in bed with Momma when I was little. She'd say "*Min Babe*. My best girl." That "*min*" is Norwegian for my.

Some families don't show their love for each other. Ours always did. Momma and Poppa lived on for their kids, and they had that love from their kids all their lives. When my brothers were grown up and married, and came back on visits, they'd never come into the house or leave it without hugging and kissing Momma. Two of my brothers were working there in Beaumont, and they'd stop by every morning on their way to the job and have a cup of coffee with Momma.

We gave my mother and dad plenty of headaches while we were growing up, the way kids always do. On Halloween we'd go out and do this trick-or-treat stuff. At our house Momma always had a whole dishpanful of cookies for the neighborhood kids. Some other places we'd turn on outdoor faucets and upset garbage cans and things like that.

One of our Halloween stunts was to soap the rails where the streetcar ran on Doucette Street. I used to love to run with that streetcar anyway, and see if I could beat it from stop to stop. Doucette Street was a muddy road then—they've paved it since.

We'd soap those tracks, so that the streetcar would slide and have to slow down or stop. Then we'd catch onto the back of the car, and pull the trolley pole down off the wire. The motorman would have to get out and fix it. I guess he knew he was in for it when he hit our block on Halloween night. But he probably had the same thing all the way down the line.

One Halloween I was dressed up in an old shirt and pair of pants that belonged to my brother Louis. Poppa had to work late that night, and when the streetcar came down Doucette Street, Poppa was on it. The car started to slip and slide, and he could see me running alongside it. And I slipped and fell in the mud, and almost went under the car. But all Poppa could really recognize there in the dark was Louis' clothes. So he thought I was Louis.

Poppa was furious. He jumped off that streetcar and I lit out for home. I got in and warned Louis, and he went and crawled under the porch where Poppa couldn't get at him. Louis wouldn't come out, and he wouldn't tattle on me, either. But I couldn't stand that very long. I said to Poppa, "That wasn't Louis you saw out there. It was me wearing Louis' clothes."

Then I dashed out and got under the porch. I told Louis, "You can come out now. Poppa knows it was me instead of you." And I stayed under that porch the longest time. I finally got off without a whipping. I guess that was because I'd confessed instead of letting Louis take the blame.

Even during the times when we were sort of poor, my mother would never dream of accepting any kind of charity. Those meals the Hansons used to bring were all right, because we'd all sit down and eat together. It was a sociable occasion among friends. But nobody could just give us food or clothing. Momma would tell us, "Don't you ever dare take any old clothes from anybody."

There was one time in grade school when all the girls were wearing big wide pleated skirts that would flare way out when you spun around. I wanted to make one, but I didn't have any material. Momma had gone to Port Arthur for the day to visit Mrs. Hanson. A girl named Anna Louise Mansfield across the street said I could have an old houndstooth wool skirt of hers to work on.

I took that skirt and cut it up and put more pleats in it than you ever saw. I could work our sewing machine real good. I was hurrying to get done before Momma came home. I pressed in my pleats, and the skirt turned out just fine. It was the fullest in the whole neighborhood. I was out in the front yard and down at the store, showing everybody how it would flare straight out.

When Momma got back and saw me, she said, "Babe, where did you get that skirt?"

I said, "Momma, this is Anna Louise's old skirt. I made me a flare skirt out of it."

I guess she figured I'd put so much of my own work into it that it wasn't just charity. She said, "All right. That's fine. You did a good job on it." She let me keep it, and I'll bet I wore that skirt for five years. I just loved it.

I know us kids were a lot of trouble to raise. But I think we realized more than some kids do that Momma and Poppa had it pretty hard, and that we should try to help them. What really drove it home to me more than anything else was something I did the day of Lillie's graduation from grade school. The graduation exercises were at night, and Momma sent me to the store before dinner to get some ground meat.

Going to the store on last-minute errands like that was one of my specialties. If it was just to the corner grocery, I'd get a big kick out of showing how fast I could make it. I'd run all the way and start hollering what I wanted before I even got inside the store, so they could have it ready and toss it to me as I came in the door. Then I'd run right back home, and sometimes they'd say, "What, back already? Why, you only just left."

This particular time I'm talking about, though, I had to go ten blocks to the store near the Magnolia Refinery. Momma was getting everything all ready for us to go to the graduation exercises. She was laying out clothes for Poppa and herself and the kids. And then she discovered she'd forgotten to get the meat for supper, which had to be served early if we were going to make the exercises. So she told me, "Here, go get some ground meat at the store. I need it for supper and I need it fast."

I got down there all right, and then on the way back I saw some kids playing ball in the school yard. I stopped to watch for a minute, and the next thing I knew I was in there playing myself.

I laid the package of meat down on the ground. I was only going to play a couple of minutes, but they stretched into an hour. Along came Momma down the street looking for me. I said, "I got the meat, Momma. It's right here." Then I looked where I'd left it, and there was a dog eating up the last of that meat.

Poor Momma! She couldn't quite catch me, so she picked up an old piece of rope that was lying on the ground and swung it at me. She whipped me all the way home with that rope. I was running as fast as I could go to stay ahead of her, but she could run fast too.

She cooled off in a few minutes. She never stayed mad very long. But I felt real bad about the way I'd let her down on a night when she had so much to do. I resolved that from then on I was going to do everything in my power for her.

When I was a little bigger, I'd get jobs after school. So did the others. I was in junior high school, about twelve or thirteen years old, and a girl in my class told me that kids could get work in the fig-packing plant in Beaumont.

So I went down there and got a job. I guess they didn't have any child-labor laws in Texas then. My pay was about thirty cents an hour. They'd run these figs down a trough in acid water, and you'd work in it with your hands. You'd peel the bad spots off the figs, and clean them real good, and then let them run on down.

Most of the workers there were using rubber gloves, but I didn't have any, and I had to work a while before I could buy some. So my hands got all sore. I asked if I couldn't do some other job, and they gave me one which I did like. There was this great big trough where they rolled down gallon cans or whatever size they were canning that day. I was the one who sat up top and unloaded the cans from the cases and kept a steady stream of them rolling down. When the cans got stuck, I'd come down with a great big cane and undo

26

the jam. Sometimes they'd holler, "They're coming too fast." Then I'd hold up for a while and stack a lot of cans on the rack, so I'd be all set when they were ready again.

Then I found out that I could make more money by going over to the potato gunnysack factory, where you sew up these sacks. The man there thought I was too young at first, but I persuaded him to give me a chance. He brought me a bunch of sacks to start on, and I said, "Bring me a couple more. I don't want to have to wait when I get through with these." He said that one bunch would be enough to hold me for a while, but I insisted, and finally he gave me some more.

It was piece work—a penny a bag, or something like that. I could sew up those sacks faster than anybody else. I was making sixty-seven, sixty-eight cents an hour. The boss knew I was interested in sports, and he told me, "Any time you want to take off and play, go ahead." So I did, and then I'd work overtime and everything to make up for it.

I'd keep a nickel or a dime for myself out of what I made, and put the rest in Momma's sugar bowl. I'd tell her, "I don't want you to spend it on groceries or anything like that. I want you to buy little things for yourself." But she never did. She saved all of it for me, and when the time came that I needed something, she'd have the money right there.

Before I was even into my teens, I knew exactly what I wanted to be when I grew up. My goal was to be the greatest athlete that ever lived. I suppose I was born with the urge to get into sports, and the ability to do pretty well at it. And my dad helped to swing me in that direction. He followed the sports news in the papers, and he'd talk to us about it. I began reading the sports pages when I was very young myself. I can remember that even then I was interested in the famous

27

golfers—the men like Walter Hagen and Bobby Jones, and the women like Joyce Wethered and Glenna Collett and Virginia Van Wie.

In the summer of 1928 the Olympic Games were being held in Amsterdam, Holland. Poppa kept reading about the Olympics in the newspapers, and telling us about the star athletes over there.

I got all steamed up. I was fourteen years old at the time. I said, "Next year I'm going to be in the Olympics myself."

Poppa said, "Babe, you can't. You'll have to wait four years."

I said, "Well, why? Why can't I be in it next year?" And he explained to me that the Olympic Games were held four years apart.

It sounded like the greatest thing in the world to me—that free trip across the ocean and everything. I didn't know that the 1932 Olympics would be held in this country in Los Angeles—not that it would have made much difference to me. Lillie and I started in training for the Olympics right then and there.

She was a tomboy in those days too. One night my brother Louis was escorting Lillie and me to a school dance. Some rowdy kids jumped out of an alley at us. They were going to beat us up. Louis started fighting the four of them all by himself, but Lillie and I waded in there with him. We ran those kids right off.

Anyway, back in 1928 when we started thinking about the Olympics, Lillie was going to be a runner and I was going to be a hurdler and jumper. I never was too good at straightaway running. I didn't seem to want to stay on the ground. I'd rather jump some obstacle.

There were hedges in the yards along our block—seven of them between our house and the corner grocery. I used those hedges to practice hurdling. But there was one of them that was higher than the others. I couldn't get over it. That sort of messed up my practicing. So I went to the people who lived in that house. Their name was King. I asked Mr. King if he'd mind cutting his hedge down to where the rest of them were, and he did it.

You're supposed to put your leg out straight when you hurdle. But a regular hurdle is just half an inch or three-quarters of an inch thick. These hedges were about two feet across. So I had to crook my left knee—that was the leg I always took off on—or I'd scratch myself up. That style of hurdling stayed with me. When I did get to the Olympics they tried to have me change, but I wouldn't do it.

I'd go flying over those hedges, and Lillie would race alongside me on the pavement. She was a fast runner, and had an advantage anyway because I had to do all that jumping. I worked and worked, and finally got to where I could almost catch her, and sometimes beat her.

I didn't beat her very often, though, because she had too much fight in her to want to lose. Lillie was a competitor. The whole Didrikson family was like that. All the boys were athletically inclined. Ole played on one of the first professional football teams in the state of Texas. Louis was a champion boxer in the Texas National Guard. Arthur started out to be a professional baseball player, but had to quit because of some trouble with his eye.

I don't guess I have to tell you that I was a pretty competitive type myself.

CHAPTER 3

All my life I've always had the urge to do things better than anybody else. Even in school, if it was something like making up a current-events booklet, I'd want mine to be the best in the class. I remember once I turned one in with hand-drawn maps and everything, and my teacher, Mrs. Rummell, wrote on it, "Babe, your work is beautiful. A triple plus!"

My sister Lillie had to make a current-events booklet in her class too, and she hadn't got around to it. So we erased what Mrs. Rummell had written on my book, and Lillie took it to school.

She never got to hand it in. Her teacher was Mrs. Rummell's sister, and when Lillie walked up to the desk to turn in that book, the teacher said, "Lillie, I've already seen that one, and I think Babe did a wonderful job on it."

In home economics we had cooking one time and sewing the next. In sewing class everybody had to make a dress one year, and I decided that mine was going to be the most complicated of them all. I'd already had a lot of experience sewing things at home.

The men probably won't be able to follow this, but it had a double yoke and an open collar in V-shaped form that could be opened or closed. The yoke across the front was filled with small box pleats—eight of them. The dress had short elbow sleeves. It was form-fitted down to the waist, then flared a bit at the hips. I had a little belt with it.

It was a blue-silk dress. Your hands were supposed to be immaculate in sewing class, because the dresses could not be cleaned. When I was almost finished, one little spot of oil did leak on it from the sewing machine. But it was on the inside where it didn't show. That was the dress of mine that took a prize at the Texas State Fair.

I liked the sewing, but at the beginning I didn't like the cooking part of home economics. Eventually it got pretty interesting, but at first it was mostly how to wash dishes and clean pots and pans and keep the cupboards neat. When the teacher, Miss Whitaker, left the room for a minute, I'd sneak out once in a while and go play basketball or something.

Then she caught me at it. She said, "You want a recess hour every hour, don't you?" She punished me by spanking me on the calves of the legs with a ruler. She said, "Don't ever do that again, or I'll have to spank you harder."

I know she liked me, and I liked her, except that I wasn't

enjoying the cooking class. It was just a course I had to take. I said, "You better spank me good, because I may do it again." And she looked at me and broke out laughing.

One time I really came a cropper in home economics was the day a rat got in the supply pantry. I said I'd go in there with a broom and get it. So I went in, and before I knew it, that rat had me backed into a corner. It reared up on its haunches at me. Man, all my braveness left me! I ran out of there and down the stairs. I never would go near that pantry again.

I always got pretty good marks in school, although I was more interested in the games than in the studies. The first organized team of any sort that I was on was the marching team in grade school. We'd march to band music. I was the leader, and I had a special uniform. I've always loved uniforms and band music. It gives me goose pimples to hear the music at a football game, or a military band playing something like "The Stars and Stripes Forever."

I went through Magnolia grade school in Beaumont, and then to South End Junior High. There were two junior high schools—the South End and the North End. The South End is David Crockett Junior High today. There was just the one high school, Beaumont High.

When I was in the grade school, both the junior-high and the high-school girls' basketball teams had to come over to Magnolia to practice. Today the Magnolia school is condemned. I went by there not long ago, and they had a big cyclone fence around what used to be our play yard. But in my day it was the newest and best. We had four outdoor basketball courts and a big gym inside.

When those high-school girls came over to our courts to

practice, I was just dying to get in and play with them. I'd hang around and pester them. Finally they did let me in, and I made a few scores and everything. They said they wished I was old enough and in a higher grade, so I could play on their team.

In junior high school I made the basketball team, but when I got to Beaumont High they said I was too small. All of us Didrikson kids seemed to get our growth late. Even in the Olympics, when I was eighteen, I wasn't much over five feet tall, and weighed only 105 pounds.

I couldn't accept the idea that I wasn't good enough for the basketball team. I didn't think the girls who played on it were anything wonderful. I was determined to show everybody. To improve myself, I went to the coach of the boys' team, Lil Dimmitt. I said to myself, "The men know more about basketball than the women."

I'd use my study hours to go practice basketball. I'd show the teacher that I had my homework all done, and get excused from the study hall. I'd go where Coach Dimmitt was, and say, "Coach, how about watching me for a while?" I'd worry him to death with questions about how to pivot and shoot free throws and do this and that. He took the time to help me, because he could see I was interested.

He went from Beaumont High to Baylor University. He's in the insurance business now—I saw him a few years ago at a dinner down in Texas. He could still remember how I used to get out there in a little T shirt and practice basketball. I'd be barefooted, because I didn't have any tennis shoes. He'd show me how to do different things, and encourage me, and I'd say, "Coach Dimmitt, tell those women I can play basketball!"

When the high school boys practiced, he'd tell me, "You sit down here and watch these boys play." I remember how I used to admire Raymond Alford—I met him again at that same dinner where I saw Coach Dimmitt. Raymond was the star athlete of the whole high school. He wasn't my boy friend or anything. I didn't have any boy friends then. I was just a fourteen-year-old kid, and I was too busy learning to dribble and pass and shoot baskets.

I was a junior before they finally gave me a chance on the Beaumont High girls' team. And I was the high scorer from the start. We went to different towns to play girls at other high schools, and we beat them all. I got my first newspaper write-up—a little item headed, BEAUMONT GIRL STARS IN BASKETBALL GAME. Then it was, BEAUMONT GIRL STARS AGAIN. I became all-city and all-state in basketball.

Down in Dallas, Col. M. J. McCombs saw those write-ups and decided to take a look at me. He's dead now. He was the boss of a department in an insurance firm, the Employers Casualty Company, and he also was director of the women's athletic program He put in a lot of time on it after the regular office hours. He read about me scoring thirty and forty points in these high-school games, and he wanted to see if I was good enough to help their basketball team, which had finished second the year before in the women's national A.A.U. tournament.

He went to Houston one afternoon to watch us play the Houston Heights high-school girls. This was in February 1930. I wasn't sixteen yet. That Houston Heights team was made up of big, tall girls, like the name of the school. I was still small, but I was fast, and I could run right around those girls. I scored something like twenty-six points in that game.

Trip to the Moon A tribe of Didriksons ride the moon That's Louis, Ole
and Arthur up front with sister Lillie
and me behind This was at the Beaumont fairgrounds I was six

Following a cloudburst in our neighborhood Lillie and me (with the lovely
Dutch cut) flank brothers Arthur and Louis The rest are neighbors

Making the winning broad jump in the Women's National Track Championships at Jersey City in '31 It was my medal hunting in this meet that started the sportswriters' keys clattering.

The payoff on all that hedgehopping En route to a new world's record of 11 8 seconds in the 80-meter hurdles at the '32 Games

Proud? You bet. Flanking me on the winner's platform at Los Angeles are Evelyne Hall of the U.S A and Marjorie Clark of South Africa

My first recorded game of golf with (*L to R*) Grantland
Rice, Paul Gallico, Westbrook Pegler and Braven Dyer.
Granny took me as his partner Somehow, we carried
the day

Home-coming Sister Lillie, Poppa, me and Mother in a happy mood after the '32 Olympics

I feel as bad as I look. Having learned that I'd been suspended by the National Amateur body for verbally endorsing an automobile, I watch my insurance-company basketball team. That's Colonel M. J McCombs, a fine, kind person. Also consoling me is Mrs. Henry Wood, our team mother.

Up in lights Yep, there I was, big as life as a paid entertainer
in a huge movie house in Chicago I didn't like it enough . only
because I liked golf more

Sometimes, in those early barnstorming days I wasn't sure if people
were laughing with or at me Jimmy Foxx might have been thinking,
"Go home, girl, and jerk sodas " but he was considerate.

Stan Kertes is the driving-range pro who took
me in hand when neither of us had a quarter
This was taken years later in Los Angeles.

Just before the final of the Texas State tourney in '35 That's Peggy Chandler, a swell girl I won it for my first golf victory The title was sweet . but not for long as the USGA then barred me from amateur competition.

Signing up with the Goldsmith sporting goods people to endorse a line of clubs. They sent me on tour with Gene Sarazen I could hit the ball a crooked mile

Lloyd Gullickson, Glenna Collett Vare, the Big Babe and the little one. This was at Sarasota, Florida—around '36 or '37 to judge by the skirts.

After the game Colonel McCombs came around and introduced himself, and asked if I'd like to play on a real big-time basketball team.

I said, "Boy, would I! Where?"

He said, "At the Employers Casualty Company in Dallas. We're getting ready to go into the nationals in March."

I told him that sounded great, and asked what I'd have to do. He said, "Well, see if you can arrange to get off from school, and get permission from your mother and dad to go."

"My dad's right here," I told him.

So Colonel McCombs spoke to Poppa, and Poppa said to me, "We'll have to talk this over with Momma. If you get up there in Dallas, that's a long way from home. You'd best talk to Momma about this."

Colonel McCombs drove us home to Beaumont in that big car of his. He had dinner with us—Norwegian meat balls and everything. He told Momma that he thought I could be a great basketball player, and that he'd like to have me on his team.

Momma and Poppa told Colonel McCombs that we'd think it over and let him know. After he'd gone, Momma said, "*Min Babe,* do you want to go way up to Dallas?"

I said, "Yeah, Momma, I want to go."

She turned to Poppa. "Oolie mon," she said—that was what her pronunciation of his name sounded like, "what do you think?"

He said, "I think it might be good for Babe."

There was a lot of talking. Momma thought I was too young to be making a trip like that, but Poppa said he'd travel along with me. Finally Momma said all right.

It was arranged that I should play out the season with

the Employers Casualty Company, then come back to Beaumont and finish up at high school. The school let me take three weeks out there to play basketball because my marks were good. I had a B plus average, as I remember.

I've told you about my train trip to Dallas, and how Colonel McCombs met us with his car at the station. He had one of the basketball girls with him, Leona Thaxton. She was a big guard. We drove to the company's offices in the Interurban Building. I remember that we went to Room 327. That's where Colonel McCombs' department was. Practically all the basketball players worked there. I guess that was to make it easier to round them all up and take off when there was a basketball trip.

I'd never seen so many large girls—large feet, and large hands. They were really husky. That was a great era of women's athletics. Nowadays the big sports for women are tennis, fancy diving, swimming and golf. And those are the best sports for women—some of the others are really too strenuous for girls. But back there in the 'thirties they made a big thing out of sports like women's basketball.

Colonel McCombs introduced me to all the girls. One of them, Lalia Warren, said, "What position do you think you're going to play?"

So I got a little pepped up there, and I said, "What do *you* play?"

She said, "I'm the star forward."

I said, "Well, that's what I want to be." And that's how it worked out, too.

Colonel McCombs asked me what kind of office work I could do. I told him I knew typing and shorthand. I'd taken that in high school. I wanted to be an athlete, but I didn't suppose then that I could make a living out of it, except maybe in physical education. I thought I might wind up being a secretary. I won a gold medal in school for hitting the best speed on the typewriter. I think it was eighty-six words a minute. I practiced by typing out "The Story of My Life." I was only fourteen or fifteen, and that story ran 42,000 words!

Anyway, Colonel McCombs asked if I could work a slide rule. I said, "No, but if it's numbers I can learn it quick." And they wound up assigning me to a job where I used a slide rule.

Then they had me pick out a basketball uniform for myself. I'd always had No. 7 in high school. I went through the extra uniforms, and there was No. 7 waiting for me. Everything seemed to be working to my pattern. The pants and shirt were too big for me, but I could sew them to fit all right. I just took the shirt in at the seams a little bit. And I tucked the pants in and made them fit skin tight, the way I liked my basketball pants. I was in great condition as a kid. There wasn't an ounce of fat on me.

I went right into a game that first night. We played the Sun Oil Company girls, the defending national champions, in a pre-tournament game. They had some pretty tough guards. They'd heard about me, and they weren't going to let this little kid from Beaumont do any shooting at all. They started hitting me that night, and they kept it up the whole season. If one guard fouled out against me, they'd send in another one.

But I broke away for my share of shots. We beat them

that first night by a pretty good score. I was the high scorer. I got four or five points more than the whole Sun Oilers' team did. From that night on I had it made.

We went on to the national tournament, and met the Sun Oilers again. This time it was a close game. At that time when a player was fouled, you could choose anyone on your team to take the free throw. We had a free-throw specialist, but late in the game, when we got a foul shot, she and the other veteran players said to me, "Here, you take it."

So I stepped up to the line, not thinking about it especially, and missed the shot. It turned out that we lost the game by one point. I really felt bad about the whole thing, even though at the end of the tournament I was chosen for the women's All-American basketball team.

I was an All-American basketball player three years in a row. The second year, 1931, we stayed at the Lasson Hotel in Wichita, Kansas, during the national tournament. Our first night there we couldn't get on the court to practice until pretty late. When we got back to the hotel, I was in such a hurry to take my shower and get to bed that I began unlacing my basketball shoes in the elevator. I kicked my shoes off as I got in the door, and pulled my socks off and tossed them in the corner.

The next day I went out and set a record by scoring more than 100 points against some Sunday School team that wasn't very good. I was superstitious about things in sports then—I've gotten completely away from that since. For the rest of the tournament, I did everything the same as the first night. I'd untie my shoes in the elevator, kick them off as I came in the room, and throw my socks in the corner.

We went all the way through and won that national

championship in 1931. We got to the finals the next year too, but lost by three points to Oklahoma Presbyterian College.

In the 1931 finals we beat a team called the Thurstons, of Wichita, 28–26. In the newspaper they ran this layout with pictures of the girls on our team. My picture was in the center, blown up way big. There were just little head shots of the others. Man, I just loved that! It was the first big publicity I'd ever had. I cut it out and sent it home to Momma. She always saved my clippings.

Anyhow, after the first national tournament back there in 1930 I went home to finish up at Beaumont High, then came back to Dallas in June to go to work permanently for the Employers Casualty Company.

I was getting $75 a month salary, and sending $45 of it home. I paid about $5 a month for a room. I wasn't spending anything on clothes. I had just the one pair of shoes, and the leather was beginning to curl. Sometimes a girl would give me one of her old dresses, and I'd cut it up and make a skirt out of it for myself.

I lived on Haines Street in the Oak Cliff section of Dallas. The basketball girls all lived in that neighborhood. We ate at the same place, Danny Williams' house. He was the assistant coach. His wife did the cooking, and she was a good cook. I can still remember her pies with graham cracker crust.

We paid 15 cents for breakfast and 35 cents for dinner. For lunch I always had toasted cupcakes and a coke down in the drugstore. The guy at the soda fountain would never charge me for my coke. He'd say, "How about another one, champ?" That made me feel good, because I wasn't any champ then.

Colonel McCombs would drive me to and from work, and

any of the other girls that wanted to go, to save us carfare. One Saturday morning at the office early that first summer he said to me, "Babe, what are you doing to occupy yourself now that the basketball season's over?" I told him I wasn't doing anything much. He said, "Well, how would you like to go out to Lakeside Park with me this afternoon and watch a track meet?"

Here I'd been thinking about the Olympic Games since 1928, and yet I never had seen a track meet. So I went out there with him, and we stood around watching. I saw this stick lying on the ground, and I said, "What's that?" Colonel McCombs said, "It's a javelin. You throw it like a spear."

He went through the motions for me, and I picked it up and tried it. I got pretty good distance, but it was so heavy— it was a men's javelin—that I slapped my back with it as I threw it, and raised a welt. Four times I slapped myself on exactly the same spot. And that welt was really big.

Colonel McCombs took me around and explained some of the other events. He showed me the high jump and the hurdles and stuff like that. Those hurdles reminded me of all the hedge-jumping I'd done back home. I liked the looks of that event better than almost anything else.

By the time we left, Colonel McCombs was agreeing with me that it would be a good idea if Employers Casualty had a women's track and field team, so the girls would have some athletics during the summer. I'm sure that's what he'd had in mind all along. He said he'd take it up with Homer R. Mitchell, the president of the company.

I told him I was going to talk to Mr. Mitchell too. Monday morning I went in and made my pitch, and Mr. Mitchell said, "Babe, whatever you all want you can have."

So we all got together and started talking about this track team we were going to organize. One girl said, "I'm going to throw the javelin." Another said, "I'm going to throw the discus." Another girl thought she'd like to do the hurdles.

When it came around to me, I said, "Colonel, how many events are there in this track and field?" He said, "Why, Babe, I think there are about nine or ten."

I said, "Well, I'm going to do them all."

Everybody nearly died laughing. I talked like that in those days, and some people thought I was just popping off. But I was serious. I said it because I thought I could do it. And in one meet we had, competing for the Texas state championship against the Bowen Air Lines girls of Forth Worth, I entered all ten events and won eight of them.

I took the three weight throws—the shot put, the discus and the javelin. I was first in both the broad jump and the high jump. I won the 100-yard dash and the 200-yard dash. In the 50-yard dash I was second. And I was on the losing team in the relay race.

I really worked hard at that track and field. I trained and trained and trained. I've been that way in every sport I've taken up. After dinner I'd go out in my tennis shoes and run. They had a hill on Haines Street that went down to a lake. I'd run all the way down there, and then I'd jog all the way back up. I'd jog my legs real high, and work my arms high, to get them in shape. Of course, they were already about as hard as they could be, but I thought they had to be better.

We had just a few days to get ready for our first meet. Our regular hour or two of practice in the afternoon wasn't enough to satisfy me. I'd go out to Lakeside Park at night and practice by myself until it got dark, which wasn't until nine or nine-thirty at that time of year. If there was good clear moonlight, I might keep going even longer.

The last night before that first track meet I went out and worked extra hard. I practiced my step timing for the broad jump and for the high jump. I put in about two hours at that, and then finished off by running the 440 yards. They'd told me to pace myself in that, but I was going to see if I couldn't sprint all the way.

Well, I just barely made it to the finish line. I fell face down on the grass. I was seeing stars. I must have laid there fifteen or twenty minutes before I could get up.

When I told Colonel McCombs about it the next morning, he said "What are you trying to do, kill yourself?" And he told me I should take it easier. But I think he admired me for working so hard.

I competed in my four events that afternoon, and I won all four. It was that last extra practice that did it, especially in the broad jumping and the high jump, where I had my steps down just right.

I eventually got to be pretty good at the high jump. I started out doing the old-style scissors jump. One afternoon I was working out, and I kept going higher and higher. Finally Colonel McCombs had the cross bar up to the women's world record. I believe it was five feet, three inches at that time.

He said, "Babe, tell you what. I'll buy you a chocolate soda if you can jump this."

I said, "Out of my way!" and sailed right over.

Then I said, "I think I can go higher." He told me to go ahead and try. I did, but I couldn't make it any more after

42

that. So we decided that if I was ever going to get above the record, I'd have to switch from the scissors jump to the Western roll, which wasn't too common then. In the Western roll you kick up there and roll over the bar flat. Under the high-jump rules they had at that time, your feet had to go over the bar first.

I was the longest time mastering that Western roll. In the beginning I'd just dive. I'd go over head first and my feet would kick up in the air and my body would knock the bar off coming down. But Colonel McCombs kept working with me, and I kept practicing, until I was sliding laterally and bringing my whole body over just the way you were supposed to.

We went in for other things besides track in Dallas there during the summers. One of the earliest items in my scrapbooks says, "An exhibition of fancy diving and swimming stunts will be given at White Rock municipal pool Sunday afternoon from 3 until 5 o'clock by Mildred Didrikson and her Employers Casualty girls. In addition the Babe will drive a motor speed boat in some fancy arcs and later will show the populace how to handle the bounding and treacherous aquaplane "

I didn't care too much for just swimming, but I did go for that fancy diving. I won diving events in swimming meets, and I honestly think I could have qualified for the Olympic swimming team if I had concentrated on it. I used to do the double gainer off the regular board, and sometimes the two-and-a-half gainer. I've done three gainers off the ten-foot platform. And my optional dive was a stand-sitting-stand where I'd finish up by turning around on the board and doing a back flip into the water.

We also had a team in a girls' softball league there in Dallas. I hit something like thirteen home runs in one double-header. Those girls weren't very good fielders, and if you hit the ball between them it would roll a long way. I was fast enough to get around the bases before they could throw it back in.

One thing that got us all started on track and field in 1930 was the fact that the women's national A.A.U. championships were going to be held in Dallas that summer on the Fourth of July. I got in there and won the javelin throw and the baseball throw. I also broke the world's record in the broad jump with a leap of eighteen feet, eight-and-a-half inches. Then Stella Walsh came along a few minutes later and took first place away from me by jumping a quarter of an inch farther than that.

In 1931 the championships were held in Jersey City. I was the leading scorer with three first places. I won the broad jump this time, although I didn't beat the record. And I did set records in winning the baseball throw with a heave of 296 feet, and the 80-meter hurdles with a time of 12 seconds flat.

But 1932 was the summer when I was really keyed up about track and field. That was an Olympic year. The national championships and the Olympic tryouts were being combined. So the ones who came out ahead in the nationals would also get to be in the Olympics. There were a lot of different events that I wanted to compete in.

I was sitting in the office one day thinking about it when Colonel McCombs buzzed for me. My call was two longs and two shorts—dah-dah-dit-dit. Colonel McCombs buzzed for me often. He'd call me in to work out basketball plays with him and things like that.

So I went into his office. I said, "Colonel, will I get to go up to Chicago for the nationals this year?"

He said, "Yes. That's what I wanted to talk to you about. I've been studying the records of the girls on the other teams that will be in the meet. I think if you enter enough different events, and give your regular performance, you can do something that's never been done before. I believe we can send you up there to represent the Employers Casualty Company, and you can win the national championship for us all by yourself."

CHAPTER 4

Once when I was playing in the Celebrities Golf Tournament in Washington a few years ago, they put me on a program with Hildegarde the singer. We were up there at the microphone talking, and she said, "Babe, I can't understand why I don't hit a golf ball as far as you do. It seems to me I swing my club the same way."

I said, "Hildegarde, it's not enough just to swing at the ball. You've got to loosen your girdle and really let the ball have it!"

That line has probably been quoted as much as anything I ever said, although when writers have used it since, they've generally had me saying it to the reporters right after winning some big tournament or other. The stories about me sometimes get a little tall in the telling.

Anyway, that girdle crack was meant as a gag, and yet there was a lot of truth in it. My main idea in any kind of competition always has been to go out there and cut loose with everything I've got. I've always had the confidence that I was capable of winning out.

One time I really needed my confidence was when Employers Casualty sent me up to Chicago as a one-girl track team for those combined 1932 national championships and Olympic tryouts. The meet was being held at Dyche Stadium, the Northwestern University field, which is in Evanston, just outside Chicago.

I never can recite all the details of my performance that afternoon without checking the record book, but I can tell you everything that happened the night before in my hotel room in Chicago. I couldn't sleep. I kept having severe pains in my stomach. When I put my hand on it, the hand would just bounce up and down.

Mrs. Henry Wood was chaperoning me. She was our "team mother" at Employers Casualty. Naturally she wasn't doing any sleeping either, the way I was tossing around. She got worried and called the hotel doctor. She was afraid I might be coming down with an appendicitis attack or something.

The doctor came and examined me. He said, "There's nothing wrong with her. She's just all excited. The excitement is affecting the nerve center in her diaphragm." And that's what it was. I've found out since that whenever I get all keyed up like that before an event, it means I'm really ready.

We finally did fall asleep around dawn. And then we

overslept. When we woke up, there was barely time for us to get ourselves ready and make it out to Evanston for the start of the meet.

We got down to the front of the hotel as quick as we could, and jumped into a taxicab. But when we told the driver we wanted to go to Dyche Stadium, he wouldn't take us. He said he just operated in Chicago.

So we got out of that cab and tried another one. This driver agreed to go to Evanston. What with the traffic and everything, though, it began to look like there wouldn't be time for me to dress out at the field. There was only one way we could make sure. Mrs. Wood held up a blanket around me and I changed into my track suit while we were riding along in the cab.

In spite of all those difficulties, it was one of those days in an athlete's life when you know you're just right. You feel you could fly. You're like a feather floating in air. I wasn't worried about the fact that of the ten individual events on the program I was entered in eight, including a couple I'd hardly ever done before, the shot put and the discus throw. I was going to be in everything but the fifty-yard and 220-yard dashes.

Mrs. Wood and I just did get there in time for the opening ceremonies. They announced each team over the loudspeaker, and then the girls on that team would run out on the track and get a hand. There were over 200 girls there. Some of those squads had fifteen or more girls. The Illinois Women's Athletic Club had twenty-two.

It came time to announce my "team." I spurted out there all alone, waving my arms, and you never heard such a roar.

It brought out goose bumps all over me. I can feel them now, just thinking about it.

Some of the events that afternoon were Olympic trials. Others were just National A.A.U. events. But they all counted in the team point scoring. So they were all important to me if I was going to bring back the national championship for Employers Casualty.

For two-and-a-half hours I was flying all over the place. I'd run a heat in the eighty-meter hurdles, and then I'd take one of my high jumps. Then I'd go over to the broad jump and take a turn at that. Then they'd be calling for me to throw the javelin or put the eight-pound shot.

Well, there were several events I didn't figure to do too much in. One was the 100-meter dash, and I drew a blank there, although I just missed qualifying for the finals. I was edged out for third place in my semifinal heat.

But that was the only thing I got shut out in. Even in the discus, which wasn't a specialty of mine at all, I placed fourth to pick up an extra point. And I actually won the shot put, which was a big surprise. A girl named Rena Mac-Donald was supposed to be the best woman shot putter, but I beat her out with a throw of thirty-nine feet, six-and-a-quarter inches.

I won the championship in the baseball throw for the third straight year. My distance was 272 feet, two inches. Then in three Olympic trial events I broke the world's record. In two of them it was a case of beating a record that I already held myself. I threw the javelin 139 feet, three inches, which was nearly six feet better than my old mark of 133 feet, five and-a-half inches. I won an eighty-meter hurdle heat in 11.9

seconds, a tenth of a second faster than my previous mark. In the finals of the eighty-meter hurdles I didn't do quite that well, but my time of 12.1 seconds was good enough to win.

In the high jump I was competing against a very fine specialist, Jean Shiley. When everybody had been eliminated except us two, they moved the bar up just a fraction above the world's record, held by a Dutch girl, Fraulein M. Gisolf. She'd cleared five feet, three-and-one-eighth inches. Now they had Jean Shiley and me try it at five feet, three-and-three-sixteenths inches. Jean and I both got over. Neither of us could make it any higher that day, so we wound up in a first-place tie.

When I came off the field at the end of the afternoon, all puffing and sweating, Mrs. Wood was so happy and excited she was crying. She said, "You did it! You did it! You won the meet all by yourself!"

Colonel McCombs had that track meet doped out just about right. Of the eight events I entered, I placed in seven. I won five of them outright, and tied for first in a sixth. I scored a total of thirty points, which was plenty to win the national championship for Employers Casualty. The Illinois Women's Athletic Club was second with twenty-two points.

George Kirksey, who covered the meet for the United Press, said it was "the most amazing series of performances ever accomplished by any individual, male or female, in track and field history." Other sportswriters were saying the same sort of thing. This was when that stuff about me being a "super athlete" and a "wonder girl" started up.

Some friends took Mrs. Wood and me out that night,

and we danced until three o'clock in the morning. If I'm not mistaken, I had myself a workout the next day, to make sure that my muscles didn't tighten up or anything. I didn't need any rest in those days. I was just an eighteen-year-old kid. It got different later on, what with my cancer operation in 1953 and the back trouble I developed in the spring of 1955 and everything.

I've come back and won my share of golf tournaments, but a lot of the time recently I've felt I'd rather be at home with my husband, George Zaharias, working around the new house we built in Tampa, Florida.

George is the business head of the family, and for a while there he wasn't sure whether we should build. Then one morning at five o'clock, here's my big bear of a husband shaking me awake. "Honey," he says, "I've been thinking it over. You can have your house."

Anyway, winning that 1932 national-championship track meet singlehanded was the thing that first made my name big—that and the Olympic Games that followed. There were only five individual track and field events for women on the Olympic program that year. I was in three of them, which was the most they would allow one person to enter. I was in the javelin, the hurdles and the high jump.

The Olympics were held in Los Angeles a couple of weeks after the tryouts. We went out there in advance to start training. Mrs. Wood came back to Dallas with the trophies I'd won in Chicago, while I got on a train for Los Angeles with the other girls who had made the Olympic team.

I wasn't getting to sail across the ocean, the way I'd dreamed of doing when I first heard about the Olympic Games back in 1928. But a trip to Chicago, and then to Los

Angeles, was almost the same as going overseas to me. I was as thrilled as any kid could be.

On the train going out, most of the girls sat around watching the scenery and playing cards and gabbing. I was busy taking exercises and doing my hurdle bends and stuff. I'd practice in the aisle. Several times a day I'd jog the whole length of the train and back. People in the other cars took to calling out, "Here she comes again!"

Other girls would say to me, "Why don't you take it easy for a while?" But I'd had my heart set on being in these Olympics for a long time. I wanted to be sure I was in shape now that I was finally getting there.

We had a stopoff in Denver so everybody could get off the train and work out. I was looking forward to seeing "The Mile High City." I was very young then, and hadn't been around much. I didn't realize the slogan came from the fact that Denver is a mile above sea level. It sounds silly now, but I expected to see a city that was built a mile up in the air.

They took us to a stadium there in Denver, and everybody went through their paces. I couldn't understand why I kept getting winded much quicker than I usually did. They explained to me that it was the effect of the high altitude. Years later Denver became my home for several years, and I found out that the altitude made a difference in the kitchen too. On a lot of dishes you couldn't go by the cooking times the ordinary recipe book called for. You had to make adjustments for that thinner air.

From Denver we went straight on to Los Angeles, and settled down there for regular workouts. The coach of the Olympic women's track and field squad was a man named George Vreeland. He wanted to improve my form in some of the events. I've told you how going over the hurdles, I bent my front leg more than you were supposed to, on account of having practiced over those hedges back home. And I didn't throw the javelin quite the way they said you should.

But I told the coach I was sorry, I wasn't going to change. My own coach, Colonel McCombs, had told me I should stick to my natural style. And I know today that he was right. There's no one way to do anything in athletics. You have to find the way that works best for you.

I don't believe Mr. Vreeland was too happy about my refusing to take any new instruction from him. But he accepted the situation. And he did say he admired my loyalty to the teachings of my coach.

While I was out there I got to meet a number of the Hollywood stars I'd seen on the screen. There was Clark Gable—he could really keep you laughing. And I spent some time with Will Rogers too. He was another wonderful fellow. Then there was Janet Gaynor and Norma Shearer and Norma Talmadge and Joe E. Brown.

It was a wonderful thrill to march into the Olympic Stadium in the parade on opening day, Monday, August first. To tell you the truth, though, I couldn't enjoy the ceremonies much after we got out there. We all had to wear special dresses and stockings and white shoes that the Olympic Committee had issued to us. I believe that was about the first time I'd ever worn a pair of stockings in my life; I was used to anklets and socks. And as for those shoes, they were really hurting my feet.

We had to stand there in a hot sun for about an hour and a quarter while a lot of speeches and things went on. My feet were hurting more and more. Pretty soon I slipped my feet out of my shoes. Then another girl did. By the end I think everybody had their shoes off.

They also issued us track shoes, but there I got permission to wear my own, which were all broken in and fitted me just right.

I was in the javelin throw that first day, and it didn't get started until late afternoon. Shadows were coming up over the stadium, and it was turning pretty cool. We all got out there to warm up. I was watching the German girls, because they were supposed to be the best javelin throwers. I could see that they'd been taught to loosen up by throwing the spear into the ground. I'd been told myself that this was the way to practice, but I never could agree. It seemed to me that this gave you the wrong motion. You'd feel a tug that wasn't right. I always thought you should warm up with the same swing you used in competition.

There were too many of us around for me to risk throwing any spears up into the air the way I wanted to. Rather than have no warm-up at all, I thought I'd practice that other way, throwing the javelin into the ground. I tried it, and I almost put it in a German girl's leg. I decided I'd better stop.

The event started. They had a little flag stuck in the ground out there to show how far the Olympic record was. It was a German flag, because a German girl had set the record. It was some distance short of my own world's record.

When my first turn came, I was aiming to throw the javelin right over that flag. I drew back, then came forward and let fly. What with the coolness and my lack of any real warm-up, I wasn't loosened up properly. As I let the spear go, my hand slipped off the cord on the handle.

54

Instead of arching the way it usually did, that javelin went out there like a catcher's peg from home plate to second base. It looked like it was going to go right through the flag. But it kept on about fourteen feet past it for a new Olympic and world's record of 143 feet, four inches.

In practice I'd made throws of close to 150 feet. Nobody knew it, but I tore a cartilage in my right shoulder when my hand slipped making that throw. On my last two turns, people thought I wasn't trying, because the throws weren't much good. But they didn't have to be. My first throw stood up to give me the gold medal for first place. A German girl, E. Braumiller, who was the defending Olympic champion in the event, came within nine inches of equalling me to place second. Another German girl, T. Fleischer, was third.

Two days later we had the qualifying heats for the eighty-meter hurdles. The Olympic record here was 12.2 seconds. The world's record, which I had set only a couple of weeks before in Evanston, was 11.9 seconds. I beat both those marks in winning my heat in 11.8 seconds.

The finals of the eighty-meter hurdles followed the next day, a Thursday. I was so anxious to set another new record that I jumped the gun, and they called us all back. Now in Olympic competition, if you jump the gun a second time they disqualify you. I didn't want that to happen, so I held back on the next start until I saw everybody taking off. It wasn't until the fifth hurdle that I caught up, and I just did beat out Evelyne Hall of Chicago. If it was horse racing, you'd say I won by a nose. Even with the late start, I set another new record with a time of 11.7 seconds.

Now all I needed was to win the high jump the next day to make a clean sweep of my three events. The high jump turned into another contest between Jean Shiley and myself, like the one we'd had in the Olympic tryouts. Both of us were better this day than we'd ever been. The cross bar moved up to five feet, five inches, which was nearly two inches higher than the record Jean and I had set in Evanston. We both cleared it. Now I'd beaten the world's record in all three of my Olympic events.

But there was still first place to be settled between Jean and myself. Since we were jumping off a tie, it was on a basis of one try only. They raised the bar another three-quarters of an inch. Jean Shiley gave it a real effort, but just missed getting across.

I took my turn. I went into my Western roll, kicking up and rolling over. I just soared up there. I felt like a bird. I could see that bar several inches beneath me as I went across. I was up around five-ten, higher than I had ever been, and it was a sensation like looking down from the top of the Empire State building. And then as I hit the ground, the bar came down after me.

Grantland Rice, who kept featuring me in his stories before and during the Olympics, described what happened this way. "There was a wild shout as Miss Didrikson cleared the cross bar by at least four inches. It was the most astonishing jump any woman ever dreamed about. But luck was against her. As the Babe fluttered to earth her left foot struck the standard a glancing blow, just six inches from the ground —and the cross bar toppled into the dust with her."

So they dropped the bar down to five feet, five-and-a-quarter inches to give us one last chance to break our first-place tie. Well, my Western roll was a little confusing to the judges. They weren't used to seeing it, especially with women jumpers. And the Western roll had to be performed just right to conform with the high-jump rules of the day. Your feet had to cross the bar first. If your head went over first, then it was a "dive" and didn't count.

We took our last jumps. Jean Shiley made hers this time. I made mine too. Then all of a sudden the judges disallowed my jump. They ruled that I had dived. Today it wouldn't matter which part of me went over first. You're allowed to get over the bar any way you possibly can, as long as you take off from the ground on one foot. But back there in 1932, the rule cost me my first-place tie.

There was a picture taken of that jump, and I think it proves my feet actually went over just ahead of the rest of me. I'd been jumping exactly the same way all afternoon— and all year, for that matter. I told the judges so, but they said, "If you were diving before, we didn't see it. We just saw it this time."

Up in the press box Grantland Rice could tell what was happening. He talked to me right afterwards, and said he thought I'd been given a bad deal. So did some of the other writers. That made me feel a little better about winding up in second place.

Then Grantland Rice gave me something new to think about. He invited me to play golf with him and some sports-writer friends out at the Brentwood Country Club. I was almost more excited about that than I had been about the Olympics themselves.

CHAPTER 5

It's sometimes hard for me to pin down the exact date when I first took up a sport. Golf is an example. I was having lunch a while back with Lloyd Mangrum and a couple of other golfers, and Lloyd said, "Babe, do you remember when you were living in Dallas, and you came out to the El Tivoli Golf Club with some friends? You were just going to walk around the course with them, but they said, 'Why don't you try a few holes?' So you borrowed their clubs and played about five holes. Then you quit and said it was a silly game."

I told Lloyd I did remember that.

"Well," he said, "do you remember who your caddy was that day?"

I stopped a moment. "Lloyd!" I said. "It was you!" And it was.

Then another time after I first came to Dallas, Colonel McCombs drove me home one Saturday afternoon, the way he so often did. I'd been practicing basketball or track—I forget which. I remember I was still in my sweat suit and tennis shoes. Anyway, Colonel McCombs said, "Babe, do you mind if I stop at a driving range on the way home and hit a few golf balls?"

I told him to go right ahead. I believe I added something about how silly I thought it was for people to hit a little white ball and then chase it. I was talking the way kids will talk when they don't know how to do something, and so they pretend they're not interested in it.

I don't suppose for a minute that I fooled Colonel Mc-Combs. I imagine his whole idea was to get me thinking about golf, just as he'd taken me out to that track meet when I first moved to Dallas.

We stopped at the driving range, and Colonel McCombs hit a few drives. Finally he invited me to try one. Or maybe I asked him to let me do it. I took my stance in front of a light post. I reared back and swung with all my might. I caught that ball square, but I came around so hard that the club hit the light post on the follow through and broke in two.

The little Scotsman who ran the driving range came running up to us. He was shouting. I thought he was mad because I'd broken the club. But instead of that he was yelling, "Wow! Look at that! See where she hit the ball!" They measured it, and it was about 250 yards.

But I don't think you could count either of those times I've mentioned as actually playing golf. So when Grantland

Rice invited me out to the Brentwood course during the Olympics, I'd never played a round of golf in my life.

Granny came around in a car early in the morning and picked me up at the hotel where I was staying, the Chapman Park. He had three other sportswriters with him—Paul Gallico and Westbrook Pegler and Braven Dyer. Did it make me self-conscious to be with well-known people like that? No, it's never seemed to bother me whether the people I meet are famous or not. Of course, I was glad of the chance to get to know these men. But I wasn't worried about them being big-name writers. All I was worried about was how good they were as golfers. I didn't want to look like a fool on that golf course.

While they were having some coffee before we teed off, I excused myself. I said I wanted to change my shoes and borrow some clubs. That wasn't all I wanted. I ducked out to the pro shop and hunted up Olin Dutra, the Brentwood pro, who won the PGA championship that year.

I said, "Mr. Dutra, I'm going to play golf with Granny Rice and Pegler and the boys. I want you to show me how it's supposed to be done so I won't look too bad out there."

He lent me some clubs, and he showed me as much as he could in a few minutes about the grip and the stance and the swing. He demonstrated how you should pivot when you swing. And he kept telling me, "Look at the ball real hard. That's the most important thing."

Finally we went out to play our round. Granny Rice was taking me as his partner because I was the beginner, while he was considered the best player of the group. We stood the other three. It was a best-ball match, so he'd have a chance to win for our side even if I didn't do any good.

I said to him, "I don't know how to play this game. So don't bet too much money!" He told me they were just going to play a dollar nassau.

We flipped a coin, and Granny and I won the toss, so I was the first to drive off. I just put my ball down and was going to hit it right off the ground, but Granny said, "Hey! You have to tee up the ball before you drive." And he teed up my first ball for me, which I've always felt was quite an honor.

I drove, and the ball sailed straight out there about 240 yards. I outdrove all the men on that first hole. They'd thought I was a great natural athlete, and wanted to see how I'd do at a new sport. But after that first drive, they couldn't believe I'd hardly ever swung a club before. They said, "You must have played a lot of golf."

A majority of my drives that day were between 240 and 260 yards. Of course, I had some bad shots in between. I've read since that my score for the round was eighty-six. Actually I think it was around 100.

Grantland Rice was playing good golf, so he and I were ahead. As I remember, we were two up coming into the sixteenth hole. That was a short hole. There was a big dip down from the tee, and then the green was way up on top of a hill.

Paul Gallico hit the best tee shot. It looked like he was a cinch to win the hole. So Granny whispered to me, "Babe, why don't you challenge Paul to race you down and up that hill?" Paul's a real good sport, and he took the dare. Of course I beat him, because I was in the peak of condition, but he raced me all the way. He was so winded he had to lie down on the grass and catch his breath. When he finally got up, he four-putted the green. Granny and I won the hole and the match.

I'd thought about being a golfer before, but I think that was the day that really determined me on it. Grantland Rice told me, and wrote in his column, that he'd never seen a woman who could hit a golf ball the way I did, and that I had the ability to be a great player.

I got in a few more licks with a golf club at the Wilshire driving range before I left Los Angeles. And I collected a few Olympic souvenirs—banners that were hanging outside buildings, and stuff like that. A story got in the paper that the "wonder girl" had been climbing up eight-story buildings to get herself some Olympic flags. Well, it wasn't quite like that. It wasn't just me doing it. It was a bunch of us girls. And we didn't scale any outside walls. We went up inside the buildings to where we could reach out and grab what we wanted.

Finally it was time to come home. I flew back from Los Angeles to Dallas. I've always remembered that plane as a big airliner. Not long ago I saw a picture of it, and it was just a little old one-engine plane that couldn't have carried more than seven passengers.

When we landed at the airport in Dallas, the mayor and everybody was there to greet me. There were a lot of civic officials, and the Employers Casualty people—Homer R. Mitchell, Colonel McCombs, Mrs. Henry Wood. They'd brought Momma and Poppa in for the welcome-home celebration too.

They paraded me through the city. One of the Dallas newspapers said the next day, "It was not unlike the reception Col. Lindbergh received when he came here after his epochal flight across the Atlantic. Paper bits and confetti, tearings from telephone books, city directories and newspapers flew from office windows."

I was riding in an open car, waving to everybody and having a whale of a time. I had chill bumps all over that whole day. They took me to the Adolphus Hotel. They had a suite of rooms for me, with flowers all over the place. But what really caught my eye was a great big watermelon that some Texan had sent. I believe it weighed 125 pounds. I stepped into the suite, where a committee was waiting, and my first words were, "Man, that's the biggest watermelon I ever saw!"

Everybody howled. We had a party later on, and more than 100 of us ate off that watermelon.

A few days after I got home, I had to go up to Chicago for a post-Olympic track meet they were having at Soldier's Field. They had rounded up as many as possible of the star athletes of all nations who had competed at Los Angeles. I didn't especially want to go. The celebrating after the Olympics, and all the appearances I had to make and interviews I had to give, had tired me out more than the Olympic Games themselves. But they sort of insisted that I go to this post-Olympic track meet.

You remember the trouble I had getting out to the stadium in my trip to Chicago for the Olympic tryouts earlier in the summer. Well, this time it was worse. I set out by plane, but the weather got bad, and we had to land at Parsons, Kansas. I switched to a train, after wiring them in Chicago about my change in plans.

By the time the train got in, I guess the meet had already started. They were waiting for me at the railroad station with a car with a siren. We roared through Chicago and down Michigan Avenue and over to Soldier's Field. They opened up the gates at one end of the stadium, and we drove right in.

They'd held up a couple of the women's events I was

entered in. When that car drove in, the announcer called out, "Here comes the Babe!" There was a terrific roar from the crowd.

I didn't do too many things that afternoon. I won the high jump and I was second in the discus. That was one event I hadn't even qualified for in the Olympics, but my best throw there in Chicago was good enough to have taken the Olympic gold medal out at Los Angeles. There was this Polish girl, though—Jadwiga Wajsowna—who beat me out for first place.

Then it was back to Dallas again. The show was over, or at least I thought it was. I had a letter from the Illinois Women's Athletic Club saying that if I went up there they'd get me a job paying $300 a month. I went in and showed the letter to Homer R. Mitchell, president of Employers Casualty.

He said, "Why, Babe, I think we can give you $300 a month to stay here."

I said, "Well, that's fine. Because I'd rather stay here where my friends are."

Whenever I got extra money, one of the things it always meant to me was that now I'd be able to do more for my mother and dad. I'm not trying to brag on myself. My brothers and sisters were the same way. They always did everything they possibly could. Even when they all were married and had children of their own, they never forgot what hard times Momma and Poppa had gone through to raise us seven Didrikson kids there on Doucette Street in Beaumont.

My first year in Dallas, when I was just making the $75 a month, I remember how happy I was coming home with a new radio for Christmas. I had it wrapped in a blanket. I sat up all night on the day coach from Dallas to Beaumont, hold-

64

ing that radio on my lap. I was wishing I could plug it in on the train somewhere to see if it would play.

The train got into Beaumont about six o'clock in the morning. I got out to the house and slipped in through the back door, which they always left open for the kids to use. I went upstairs to Momma and Poppa's bedroom. They were sleeping—Poppa was snoring away. I plugged the radio in right by Momma's bed and tuned in Station KFDM, where I used to hear Castor Oil Clarence when I was little. They woke up to the music on the radio, and they were so excited about it!

That radio cost me almost a month's salary, but I was able to get it on credit. For a while there, if I bought anything at all expensive, it generally had to be on credit. The people at the stores knew who I was, and they always seemed to give me a break. I might have to tell them, "I don't know just how I'm going to pay for this, but I'll do it somehow." And they'd let me take it, and I always did get it paid off.

One time in those early days I did have eighty dollars in cash saved up. Now something Momma had wanted all her life was an ivory bedroom set. I was walking past a store in Beaumont, and I saw this secondhand bedroom set—a big bed with wicker stuff in the back, and a big dresser, and two little tables. I knew Poppa could fix it all up like new.

I went in the store and asked them how much they wanted for it. They said, "A hundred dollars." I said, "I'll give you eighty dollars for it." They said all right, and I had them send it to the Ryder Furniture Company, where Poppa worked. They probably thought that was just terrible, me buying something from one furniture store and then sending it to another to be refinished.

Poppa was the boss of the refinishers at his store, and they did a beautiful job on that bedroom set. They painted it ivory just as Momma had always wanted. She loved it. It's still in the house on Doucette Street. It was sold with the house. When I went through there a while back I saw it. It's painted green now.

After I began making more money, I could do things like taking Poppa downtown to the store and buying him a new suit and a supply of the khaki pants and shirts he wore all the time.

And I loved to buy clothes for Momma. Once I took her to a store called the White House in Beaumont. I said, "Momma, pick you out a dress." She did, and I said, "Pick you out another one."

I kept on going until she had eight dresses. I said, "Momma, now you've got a dress for every day in the week and two for Sundays." She was the most tickled person you ever saw. She practically wore out those dresses showing them to everybody that came to the house.

Then there was one spring when Momma had a bad accident. She was going to a church service at night, and decided to run across a street. That was just like Momma Well, she didn't see this car coming, and it hit her. It broke her pelvis and crushed her ankle and banged up her arm.

Naturally she was in bed a long time, but she didn't stay there as long as was expected. This was in the days before they began having patients get out of bed and exercise as soon as possible. Momma was about two weeks away from being able to get out of bed—according to the doctors—when she said, "I've got to get up. I've got to see if I can walk again." And she struggled to her feet, with her arm and her ankle in casts, and her pelvis all strapped up. She started hobbling around, and she never did go back to bed again, except to rest.

Mother's Day was coming, and I wanted to do something extra nice for her. I took her down to an appliance store the Saturday before to look at mechanical ice boxes and stoves. I didn't tell her I was planning to buy them or anything. Of course the ones she liked best had to be the biggest and most expensive in the place.

I think this was the spring after the Olympic Games. I had some money at the time, but not enough to make more than a down payment on the ice box and stove I wanted. I took Momma home, then went back and explained my financial problem to the man at the store. He said, "Why don't you just wait a while until you can arrange to pay for this?"

I said, "But I can't wait! I want to get the ice box and stove out tomorrow. I want them for Mother's Day."

He said, "Well, I'll be at the store tomorrow morning. You come down and we'll see what we can do."

I was there in the morning, and he agreed to make delivery and let me pay off the balance on credit. Since it was Sunday, only a couple of the men were there. I rode out on the delivery truck to give them a hand. First I called my sister Lillie at home. I asked her to keep Momma out of the way while the delivery was being made.

Momma already had dinner cooking on the stove. We brought in the new one and they connected it up, and put the stuff that was cooking right onto it. Then they hooked up the new ice box, and loaded everything into it from the old one.

When they were all finished I gave Lillie the high sign.

Pretty soon Momma came limping into the kitchen to check on her cooking. She saw the new stove, and she couldn't believe it. Then she started over to the ice box, and saw that was new too.

She was so overwhelmed she started to cry. She came over and began hugging me. *"Min Babe!"* she kept saying. "You did it! My best girl!"

I'm telling you, I've won a lot of big prizes, but none of them ever gave me quite the same thrill I had that day.

Well, after the Olympics and the post-Olympics and all that were over, I got back into the old office and basketball routine at Employers Casualty. I was still liking it. But the pressure got pretty heavy on me during the fall of 1932. People kept telling me how I could get rich if I turned professional. That big-money talk sounds nice when you're just a kid whose family has never had very much.

What I really wanted to do at this point was to become a golfer. I was going to make an appearance at the Dallas ball park, and they were going to present me an expensive watch. I went by the Cullum and Boren sporting-goods store there in Dallas one day, and saw this beautiful set of golf clubs in the window. It was like a girl seeing a mink coat. I was just dying to have those golf clubs, but I couldn't possibly afford to buy them.

I went in and handled the clubs and everything. I know they'd have been glad to present me the golf clubs at the ball-park ceremony instead of the watch, which cost just about as much. But it might impair my amateur standing in golf if I accepted those clubs. So I took the watch instead.

Early in December of 1932 my name and picture turned up in a newspaper ad, with the statement that I liked the new

1933 Dodge automobile. The Southern branch of the Amateur Athletic Union declared me a professional. That would have been fair enough if I'd given permission for my name to be used in that ad, or taken pay for it. But I hadn't. A Dodge man in Dallas had set it up on his own. He didn't realize that it would cause any trouble.

I'd already started another basketball season with the Employers Casualty Golden Cyclones. This made me ineligible for that. And it meant I couldn't compete in the A.A.U. track meets any more, either. The Dodge man in Dallas wrote the A.A.U., explaining that I wasn't to blame, and so did the advertising agency that handled the ad. And later on that month the A.A.U. announced that it was reinstating me as an amateur.

But by then I'd decided to turn pro anyway. I started out by doing some work for the Chrysler Motor Company, which makes the Dodge car. They were sorry about what had happened, and they wanted to make it up to me. They brought me up to Detroit, with my sister Esther Nancy as chaperone, and got us a suite of rooms in the Book Cadillac Hotel. We met all the Chrysler people—the president, K. T. Keller, and everybody. And they were real nice.

They hired me to appear at the Dodge booth at the Auto Show in Detroit. I signed autographs and talked to people. I even played the harmonica to attract the attention of the crowd and draw people over to the booth.

Chrysler also got a fellow named George P. Emerson at the Ruthrauff & Ryan advertising agency to act as my agent and arrange some bookings for me. It didn't cost me anything. He got me a contract to start out making stage appearances on the RKO circuit after the Auto Show was over.

I opened with a week at the Palace Theater in Chicago. I had top billing in a stage show with Fifi D'Orsay and Bob Murphy and his Collegians. I was given the star dressing room. Somebody told me that Fifi D'Orsay didn't like that. I went to her and said, "Miss D'Orsay, I'd like for you to have my dressing room."

She said, "How sweet of you! But I wouldn't dream of it." And she didn't change dressing rooms with me, but we became good friends after that.

I'd never done any kind of theatrical performing in my life. I thought I wasn't scared until we drove up to the theater the first morning, and I saw a crowd of people lined up down the block. I said, "My Lord, I can't go through with this!"

I had an eighteen-minute act. A performer named George Libbey was working with me. He'd be up there on the stage to get things started. He'd play the piano and do an Eddie Cantor imitation. Then I'd come down the aisle wearing a real cute panama hat and a green swagger coat and high-heeled spectators. The idea was that I was just back from Florida.

We'd swap a few lines, and then I'd sing a song. It was a take-off on "I'm Fit As A Fiddle And Ready For Love." It went:

> I'm fit as a fiddle and ready to go.
> I could jump over the moon up above.
> I'm fit as a fiddle and ready to go.
>
> I haven't a worry and haven't a care.
> I feel like a feather just floating on air.
> I'm fit as a fiddle and ready to go.

70

Then when I came to the middle part I'd go "boop-boop-a-dee-dee," like Bing Crosby was doing at that time.

After I got through singing I'd sit down and take my high heels off, and put on rubber-soled track shoes. Then I'd remove my coat. I was wearing a red-white-and-blue jacket and shorts of silk satin. I'd demonstrate different kinds of athletics.

One of the things I did was run on a treadmill. They staged it real nice, with a black velvet backdrop and a great big clock to show how fast I was going. They had someone running beside me on another treadmill. At the end they would forge my treadmill ahead a little bit. I'd break the tape and go on to win.

I was surprised at how good a notice that show got the next day from Clark Rodenbach in the Chicago Tribune. This is what he said about my act:

"Friday afternoon was the 'Babe's' first time behind footlights, and the girl from the Lone Star state took the hurdle as gallantly as she ever did on the track. If her heart was thumping from the dread disease of stagefright, it wasn't apparent from the audience. After a bit of preliminary clowning by her partner, George Libbey, who was rushed here from New York for the occasion, 'Babe' sings a song over the 'mike,' and then goes into her equivalent of a dance.

"The 'Babe' skims a hurdle, jumps a couple of times, drives imitation golf balls, and runs on a treadmill. Mr. Libbey bemoans the fact that the limited scope of the stage forbids her showing more of her extraordinary prowess, such as heaving the discus, flinging the javelin or tossing a basketball. And Mildred ends her turn by playing a harmonica with no mean skill."

71

On the harmonica-playing, there were just three numbers that I'd practiced to play with the orchestra. I believe that "When Irish Eyes Are Smiling" was one of them, and "Begin the Beguine" was another. I forgot what the third one was.

One night the audience wouldn't let me off until I'd given some encores. I didn't know how I could do it, until they whispered to me from the orchestra pit, "Babe, you just go ahead with any numbers you want, and we'll fill in and make you sound good."

On my song, I could carry a tune pretty good. In fact, one of the Chicago newspaper critics didn't believe it was really me singing. He wrote that maybe they were piping in somebody else's voice while I stood in front of the microphone and went through the motions.

I got out there at one of my evening shows and said, "I see where some of these critics don't believe I'm doing my own singing. I'm going to sing tonight without a mike." So I did, and the audience gave me a real ovation.

During one show George Libbey and I were out there, and I happened to glance at the little sign at the side of the stage that showed the name of the act. He said, "What are you looking at, Babe?" and I said, "Oh, I'm just looking to see who the hell's on." That drew such a laugh that they made it part of the act from then on.

Before the week was out I was beginning to enjoy myself. I liked the feeling of that crowd out there. I had bookings after Chicago in Brooklyn and New York at something like $2500 a week.

And yet it was still in my craw that I wanted to be a champion golfer. I could see I'd never get to do that with these four and five stage shows a day. I was spending all my time either in the theater or in my hotel. And I didn't like having to put that grease paint on for every show.

I talked it over with my sister Esther Nancy—we called her Nancy. She said, "Babe, honey, you can make a lot of money on this circuit. It's just a question of whether you want to do it."

I said, "Nancy, I don't want the money if I have to make it this way. I want to live my life outdoors. I want to play golf."

Nancy agreed that it was best for me to pull out if I felt that way. She told George Emerson about it, and he understood. So we canceled the New York and Brooklyn dates. I quit after the one week in Chicago.

I've often thought since that if I hadn't pulled out then I'd still be in show business today. Because it was beginning to get in my blood. And if I'd known what tough financial times I was going to face, I'd probably have thought twice about passing up the money for those other stage bookings.

CHAPTER 6

One of the nice things about making a name for yourself in sports is that you get to meet and know the famous athletes who have been your heroes. That sort of thing started for me in the months after the Olympics.

It was during my week at the Palace Theater in Chicago that I first met Jack Dempsey. Back home in Beaumont when I was little, I can remember lying in bed one night listening to a broadcast of a Dempsey fight on the crystal set. Well, Bob Murphy, of our stage show, knew Dempsey, and brought him around to the theater to meet some of the performers.

Arch Ward of the Chicago Tribune was with them. He invited us to run up to the newspaper office with him and see what a big sports department looked like. He took us into the clipping morgue. Of course, there were several drawers full of clippings about Jack Dempsey, while my file only took up part of a drawer at that time.

Jack Dempsey walked me back to the theater. It was icy. The wind was blowing like mad. We were crossing the bridge by the Wrigley Building, and Jack said, "It's too cold just to walk. Come on, let's run." We ran, and it's a good thing we were arm in arm, because I hit an icy patch and slid. I might have slid right into the river if he hadn't held my arm. I almost went off the bridge, and he almost went with me.

Another fellow I met very early in my career was Babe Ruth. I made a point of being introduced to him, because he was the original Babe. He seemed to take an interest in me too. He said, "Babe, let me give you some advice. I wish someone had told me this when I was your age. I know you're making money. Put some of it away. Get yourself an annuity."

Babe Ruth and I were buddies for years. We'd be teamed in golf exhibitions and things like that. The last time I saw him was in Coral Gables, Florida, in 1948, a few months before his death. He didn't look well. We were playing golf for the benefit of a cancer fund drive. Here he was going to die of cancer, and I was due to come down with it, although of course neither of us knew it at the time.

I came out to the first tee with my husband George, who is even bigger and huskier than Babe Ruth ever was. Well, the Babe grabbed me and gave me a big hug and kiss. He turned to George and grinned, and said in that husky whisper he spoke in then, "What are you gonna do about it?"

After I pulled out of those stage bookings early in 1933, I went on to New York and made a few miscellaneous sports

appearances. I played a billiard exhibition with Ruth Mc-
Ginnis, a woman professional. Then I played basketball one
night in a game between two girls' teams, the Brooklyn Yankees and the Long Island Ducklings.

I played for the Brooklyn Yankees. Was that other team
ever rough! Those Long Island Duckling girls were out to
show me up. I never got pushed around and fouled so much
in any basketball game. They were determined I wasn't going
to make a single basket. They beat me all over the place.

Now there's nobody who wants to win more than I do. I'll
knock myself out to do it. But I've never played rough or
dirty. To me good sportsmanship is just as important as winning. That's one of the things my dad drummed into me. You
have to play the game the right way. If you win through bad
sportsmanship, that's no real victory in my book.

Those Long Island Ducklings sure made it tough for me.
Near the end of the first half my pants got split part way up
the side, and some of my bare skin was showing. Everybody
thought that I'd change my pants at half time. But I wasn't
going to change. I was all fired up to get back there and show
these girls they couldn't stop me with their rough stuff.

When we came out for the second half, and the people
saw me still wearing those torn pants, they cheered and
yelled, "Come on, Babe!" And I began breaking loose. On one
play I took the ball at center court and dribbled all the way
through them to score. I jumped so high and hard going in
for the basket that my arm hit the backboard, and I wound up
in somebody's lap about six rows back.

Basketball scores often ran low in that era. This was a real
low-scoring game, what with that roughhouse guarding. But

of the nineteen points our team scored, I made nine. And we held the Long Island Ducklings to sixteen points to win.

After the game they made me a presentation of a duck. It was the most beautiful thing you ever saw, with a big green ribbon on it and a big yellow bill. I didn't know what to do with it, but I wanted to keep it. I don't get rid of anything that is a gift—I value and appreciate gifts more than things I buy for myself.

I took that poor duck back with me to my room in the Congress Hotel. You can imagine what it was like. I tried to keep the duck in the bath tub, but it would get out and walk around the room.

I took it down to the desk the next morning and asked them, "Will you ship this duck home for me air express?" They said they would. And then a couple of nights later they had a country dance night at the hotel—Vincent Lopez was the orchestra leader—and I won a little white pig. The hotel shipped the pig home for me too.

Momma and Poppa were nearly going crazy back in Beaumont—ducks coming to the house, and pigs coming.

Then I went back home myself. I believe I worked for Employers Casualty for a while, and then in the spring I went out to California. This was still 1933. I was going to do nothing but learn golf. I took Momma and Poppa with me. They were both getting older, and I thought they should have a rest and a change.

I told a reporter out in Los Angeles, "I have enough money to last me three years and I intend to win the women's amateur golf championship before those three years and my bankroll are gone."

This big bankroll I was talking about was actually some such amount as $1800. I thought, "I can live forever on this. This is more money than I ever saw."

Well, I was right about it taking your full time to become a top golfer, but I soon found out that I was wrong about how long the $1800 would last. I was practicing my golf out at a driving range, trying to hold down those expenses.

Lou Nash, a golfer friend out there, got interested in me, because I was hitting such a long ball and everything. He said, "Why don't you get some pro to help you?"

I said, "What do you mean, get a pro to help me?"

"I mean you should take golf lessons," he said.

"How much does it cost?" I asked.

"Oh, they charge about three dollars an hour," he said.

"Then I can't do it," I told him. "I just can't afford it."

He said, "Let me go here and talk to a fellow a minute."

He went over and spoke to a young golf pro named Stanley Kertes, then brought him back and introduced us. I liked Stan Kertes right off the bat. He was about my age. He told me I could really hit a golf ball, but that I should take some instruction to learn basic foundation stuff.

I said, "Yeah, but it costs too much money."

He said, "I'll teach you free."

We worked there all day. Stan Kertes is a great teacher of golf—I've been going back to him ever since when I have the chance. He got me a set of clubs out of the driving-range shop. Then we started in on the grip—the correct right hand grip. And he stressed to me the importance of the firm left arm. He never drilled me to keep it dead straight. If the left arm bends just a little, that's okay, and everything will be fine with the right arm too.

78

When it got to be dinnertime, he took me out to eat. I felt kind of bad that he should give me free lessons and pay for my dinner too. When we finished I thanked him very much and said, "I'll see you."

"Do you want to quit?" he said.

I said, "No, I'd like to hit some more. But balls cost fifty cents a bucket."

"Come on," he said. We went back, and he got three or four buckets of balls. I stayed out there until twelve o'clock when they turned the lights off.

Stan told me to come back again the next day, and when I asked what time, he said, "As early as you want to." He was going to stop all his paid lessons for a while and just work with me, giving me a real fast, concentrated course.

The next morning I couldn't wait to get out there. I had my shower and breakfast and was ready to leave for the driving range by five o'clock in the morning. It wasn't daylight yet, but rather than just sit around, I went out there. I had a golf club, and I practiced what he'd told me about the grip and the stance. Finally they came and opened up the place, and Stan and I hit balls all day long.

It went on like that day after day. But eventually my money did run out. And I knew I couldn't keep on taking up all Stan's time that way with free lessons.

So by the end of the summer the Didriksons had to go back to Texas. Momma and Poppa went home to Beaumont. I went to work for Employers Casualty again. Those people were wonderful to me. There must have been four or five times when I had to come back to them, and always there was a job for me at $300 a month.

Another thing I won't forget is the automobile-accident

policy I had with them. In the periods when I wasn't working there, I never thought to pay the premiums. It was during one of those in-between times that I had an auto wreck. I reported it to Employers Casualty and said, "I suppose my policy's no good any more." They told me, "No, you're still insured. We've kept the policy up for you." And they paid the damages.

I think it was the fall after we came back from California —this was still 1933—that Poppa took sick. He needed an operation. We had no money for it. I inquired around and found that at the John Sealy Hospital in Galveston we could get it done free. Naturally it didn't occur to me that some day I might have to go into the John Sealy Hospital myself.

I came home to Beaumont to get Poppa. He was lying out on the porch where all us kids used to sleep. It shocked me to see how bad he looked. He was so sick, and he must have lost twenty-five or thirty pounds.

I said, "Poppa, do you feel well enough to ride in the car?"

"Babe, I'll do anything," he said.

So I said, "Come on, let's go to Galveston. I've got things all set up." We drove to the hospital in Galveston, and a Doctor Cohen did a fine job of operating on him.

Poppa had always been a great pipe smoker. He'd had to give that up during his illness. I know how he must have missed it, because that pipe used to be going all the time. He'd fall asleep at night, and the pipe would drop out of his mouth. He'd wake up early in the morning and light it up the very first thing. Sometimes you could hardly breathe when Poppa was in the room, the air would be so thick with smoke.

Three days after the operation Momma and I were visiting Poppa in the hospital. Momma and I had a room nearby for which we were paying fifty cents a day. We had to take the cheapest room we could find.

Doctor Cohen walked in. "Mr. Didrikson," he said, "where's your pipe?"

"I thought I wasn't supposed to smoke it," Poppa said.

Doctor Cohen said, "Get up and go sit on the porch and smoke your pipe."

"Get up?" said Poppa. "I was just operated on three days ago."

"Yes, get up and go smoke your pipe," Doctor Cohen told him. "You're all right. You can go home in a couple of days."

Poppa did get out of the hospital in another couple of days, and he began gaining back his weight and feeling good again. But it would be a while before he'd be able to work. It was up to me to earn some money. I wanted to make more than the $300 a month at Employers Casualty if I could, so I accepted an offer from a promoter named Ray Doan, of Muscatine, Iowa, to go on a basketball tour with a team he called Babe Didrikson's All-Americans.

Another girl athlete, Jane Mitchell, was with me on that team, and for a while we had a third girl on the squad. The rest of the players were men. We appeared in different cities, playing against local men's teams, and generally we made out all right. We weren't worldbeaters, but we had a pretty fair bunch of basketball players.

In the spring of 1934, after the basketball season had ended, this same promoter, Ray Doan, got me to appear with his House of David baseball team. Maybe you remember that outfit. All the players had beards. They booked games all over the country and drew some good crowds.

I was an extra attraction to help them draw the crowds. I was the only girl—and I didn't wear a beard. I didn't travel with the team or anything. I hardly even got to know the players. I had my own car, and I had the schedule, and I'd get to whatever ball park they were playing at in time for the game. I'd pitch the first inning, and then I'd take off and not see them again until the next town. As I remember, my earnings from both the basketball and the baseball were about $1000 a month.

In Florida before the baseball tour started, I did a little exhibition pitching against some of the major-league and minor-league teams. One day I was at Bradenton, Florida, where the St. Louis Cardinals were training. They were going to play an exhibition game with the Philadelphia Athletics. I was sitting in the grandstand before the game with Dizzy and Paul Dean of the Cardinals. Jimmy Foxx of the Athletics was there too.

Dizzy Dean was always bragging, you know. That is, people called it bragging. Actually, it was just his way. It was Southern Texas talk. Dizzy was good and he knew it. He'd say, "I'm gonna do something big"—and then go ahead and do it.

Well, we were talking there, and the fellows were kidding each other back and forth. There was a little ribsteak going on. And Dizzy says to Jimmy Foxx, "We'll pitch Babe against you, and I'll betcha that me and Paul and Babe can beat you guys."

So it wound up with me pitching the first inning for the Cardinals. Frankie Frisch was managing the team then, and he was a fellow to enjoy a stunt like that. Dizzy Dean wasn't in there at the start of the game, but they put Paul Dean out in left field, because he was going to come in anyway and pitch after I finished.

Pretty soon the bases were loaded with none out. Those bases got loaded on hits, not walks. I always had pretty good control. I seldom walked anybody. But I couldn't seem to throw the ball past these major-leaguers.

The next batter hit a line drive, but it turned into a double play and nobody scored. That brought up Jimmy Foxx.

There was a big grove of orange trees out back of left field. I don't suppose many balls were hit that far, but with a girl pitching and Jimmy Foxx batting, Paul Dean wasn't taking any chances. He was backed up almost to the edge of the orange grove.

And Jimmy Foxx hit a ball deep into those trees. Paul Dean turned and started running back. He disappeared right into the orange grove. A couple of moments later he came trotting out. He was holding up his glove for everyone to see. There was a baseball and about five oranges in it. That's how we made the third out. And that was enough pitching for me that day.

I guess I've competed in more different sports than any other girl, but I've always drawn the line at certain things. I never played football, although it's been printed hundreds of times that football was one of my sports, along with some other things I never did, like wrestling and boxing.

Those neighborhood touch-tag games when I was a kid were the closest I ever came to playing football. After I got my reputation as an all-around athlete in the Olympic games, Grantland Rice made a movie short of me demonstrating how I handled myself in different sports. Football was one of them.

I punted and forward-passed. Then they had me running with the ball against the SMU team. I'd zigzag down the field, and they'd keep diving for me and just miss me. It looked real good in the picture. And they had me tackle a fellow. We did it nice and easy, but they speeded up the camera so that it looked like the real thing.

As for those other rough sports, my husband George did all the wrestling in the family—he was one of the big-name professionals for many years. And on the boxing, here's what started so many people to thinking that I used to do that.

Back when I was playing basketball on the Employers Casualty team, we were in Wichita, Kansas, for the national tournament. Bill Stribling, the kid brother of Young Stribling, the heavyweight contender, happened to be in town. They called him Baby Stribling. He was a fighter too.

A photographer brought him out to the hall where our team was practicing. The photographer asked me if I'd mind putting on a pair of boxing gloves and posing with Stribling. I said sure, I'd go along with the gag. I was already in my basketball suit, so I didn't have to change clothes for the picture or anything. I've always been glad to co-operate with photographers anyway. I know the picture can help me, and help whoever else is in it, and help the photographer too.

So they tied the gloves on me, and I pretended to square off with Stribling while the photographer shot some pictures. That was all, but the story began to appear in print later on that I'd once had an exhibition sparring match with Baby Stribling. The more that story was told, the wilder it got. Some versions had me doing everything but knock him out. Actually, I've never had boxing gloves on in my life except for publicity pictures.

84

Anyhow, getting back to my baseball pitching with the House of David team in 1934, by the end of that summer I was about $3700 ahead. That bankroll didn't last long either. One reason was that I'd overdone the advice Babe Ruth gave me about taking out an annuity. When I was making $300 a month, I started paying $150 a month into an annuity. With the basketball and baseball tours, I increased the amount to $600 a month. I couldn't keep up the payments. I wound up losing my annuity altogether.

These years I'm talking about were a mixed-up time for me. My name had meant a lot right after the Olympic Games, but it had sort of been going down since then. I hadn't been smart enough to get into anything that would really keep me up there.

I had to find some way to build my name up again, so I could make some money. There had to be money—not just for me but for the family. At one point I thought maybe tennis would be the answer. I figured there could be money in that —it's a sport where you can sell tickets and people can sit down and watch you play. If I got good enough at the game, I thought perhaps a lot of people would pay to see me play tennis matches.

I don't know whether it would have worked out like that, because I never got a chance to try it. I started practicing tennis. I was learning the forehand stroke, and the backhand. Then we began on the serve, and I found I couldn't do it right. I couldn't raise my arm properly. That cartilage I'd torn in my right shoulder, throwing the javelin at the Olympic Games, still hadn't healed quite right.

The shoulder trouble didn't bother me on any of the other tennis strokes. It was just the serve that it interfered with. But that was enough to kill me for tennis, of course.

The shoulder didn't interfere with my golf swing, either. And golf was still my real objective. All I wanted to accomplish with these other things was to get in a financial position where I could concentrate on golf. That was my big sports love now.

Bobby Jones came to Texas to play an exhibition at the Houston Country Club, and I traveled all the way from Dallas to see him. He'd turned professional since making his grand slam of the British and American amateur and open tournaments in 1930. He was a great idol of mine.

I sat with Bobby at a golf writers' dinner in New York not too long ago, and I asked him if he remembered playing that exhibition in Houston. He said, "Yes, I remember. We got rained out there."

And that's what happened. He just got to play a couple of holes, and then the rain ended the round. It was such a disappointment to me. Even in the short time I got to watch him, though, I was impressed by the way he stepped up there on the tee and slugged the ball. He was out to hit the ball just as hard as he could. And that's always been my kind of golf.

I saw that Bobby Jones exhibition a short time after my summer of baseball with the House of David. Seeing Jones sort of fired up my own golf ambitions. And Employers Casualty helped to make it possible for me to get going on golf again. They not only gave me my job back one more time, they got me a membership at the Dallas Country Club and paid for my lessons there with George Aulbach.

I spent practically all my spare hours out there. In November of 1934 I decided to find out how much progress I was making by entering my first golf tournament—the Fort Worth Women's Invitation.

I went out there for the qualifying round. Somebody asked me how I thought I'd do, and I said, "I think I'll shoot a seventy-seven." I said things like that in those days, and I wasn't trying to be smart—it was just what was in my mind at the time. And that's the sort of thing that can make you famous—if it comes true.

It came true that day. I played my eighteen holes, and my score was exactly seventy-seven. That made me the medalist for the tournament—the next best score was eighty-two.

It did me good to see the headlines in the Texas newspapers the next day: WONDER GIRL MAKES HER DEBUT IN TOURNAMENT GOLF: TURNS IN 77 SCORE. It was like 1932 all over again.

I guess the qualifying medal was as much as I could expect to win my first time out. Anyway, I got eliminated in an early round of the tournament match play that followed.

Then it was winter. I was already thinking about the Texas state women's championship in the spring of 1935. That would be my next chance to establish myself as a golfer. It was terribly important to me to win that tournament. I started getting ready for it about three-and-a-half months beforehand. I settled into as tough a siege as I've ever gone through for any sports event in my life.

CHAPTER 7

I've competed in national and international championships where the name of the winner gets flashed around the world. But no prize I've won, either before or since, looked any bigger to me than the Texas state women's golf championship did when I took aim on it in 1935.

The tournament was scheduled for late April. I started practicing for it in January. I still had plenty to learn. There'd been too many interruptions in my golf playing for me to have mastered the game yet.

Weekends I put in twelve and sixteen hours a day on golf. During the working week I got up at the crack of dawn and practiced from 5:30 until 8:30, when I had to leave for the office. I worked until lunch time, then had a quick sandwich and spent the rest of my lunch hour practicing in the boss's office, which was the only one that had a carpet. He told me it was all right to do it.

I practiced putting on the carpet, and I chipped balls into his leather chair. They moved the chair over into a corner for me, away from the window. And I stood in front of the mirror on his closet door and practiced my grip. I watched to see whether I had it exactly the way Stan Kertes and George Aulbach had told me.

When the lunch hour was over, I went back to work until 3:30. After that I was free to go out to the golf course. George Aulbach would give me an hour's instruction. Then I'd drill and drill and drill on the different kinds of shots. I'd hit balls until my hands were bloody and sore. I'd have tape all over my hands, and blood all over the tape.

After it got too dark to practice any more, I went home and had my dinner. Then I'd go to bed with the golf rule book. I'll bet I have read that book through twenty-five times, line by line. Today when I'm playing with anybody and a rule question comes up, they say, "Ask Babe."

There've been times when I've almost wished I didn't know the rules so well. In 1946 I was at Spring Lake, New Jersey, playing in the Spring Lake Women's Open. I started out in the qualifying round and shot the first four holes in one under par. On the fifth hole my tee shot sliced off into the rough. I went over there and played out a nice iron shot to the green.

I finished that hole, and the sixth one. After holing out on the sixth green, I walked over to the ball washer, and all of a sudden I saw that I had a strange ball in my hand. I'd mistaken it for my ball in the rough back there on the fifth hole.

I said to the other girls in my foursome, "Well, that's it. I've been playing the wrong ball. I've disqualified myself."

Nobody else ever would have known the difference if I'd kept quiet about it. But I'd have known the difference. I wouldn't have felt right in my own mind. You have to play by the rules of golf, just as you have to live by the rules of life. There's no other way.

Anyhow, the importance of studying the rules was something both Stan Kertes and George Aulbach stressed when I was learning golf. So in my preparations for that 1935 Texas state women's championship, I wanted to be sure that I wouldn't beat myself because of not knowing some of the rules.

The tournament was being held at the River Oaks Country Club in Houston, and I was allowed to go over there a little ahead of time. I went to Houston with my friend Bertha Bowen of Fort Worth—she and her husband, R. L. Bowen, have always been like a godmother and godfather to me.

I got in some practicing out at the River Oaks course. Jack Burke, the pro there, helped me. He's one of so many fine men I've been indebted to over the years for showing me how to improve my golf.

I'd come in after finishing a round, and he'd say, "How did you do?" I might say, "I got a pretty good score today, but I wasn't hitting that No. 3 iron too good." He'd say, "Well, let's work on it a little." And he'd come out and work with me.

He died several years ago. His son, Jack Burke, Jr., is one of the name golfers on the men's professional circuit today. Jackie was just a growing boy at the time I'm talking about, but he was already a pretty fair golfer. Young Jackie and I would get out there and play together. I wasn't going to let any kid hit the ball farther than I did, and he wasn't going to let any girl beat him. Each of us would try to outslug the other.

I always liked to play golf with men and boys. In fact, people advised me to do it. I was told that it would be better competition for me, and that I'd learn more by trying to hit the ball the way the men did. I think that practicing so much with the men is one of the reasons why I became a long hitter.

After a week or more of working out at River Oaks, I was ready for the qualifying round on April twenty-second. This was a tournament for women amateurs, of course. Maybe you're wondering how I could play in it if I was a professional athlete. Well, I was a professional with the Amateur Athletic Union in the women's sports they governed, like basketball and track. But I'd never been a professional in golf, where the amateur body is the United States Golf Association. Bertha Bowen helped me on my entry for this tournament, and it went through without any trouble.

So play began. I qualified all right, although I didn't head the list the way I had in my other tournament. I shot an eighty-four. The medal was taken by Mrs. Dan Chandler— Peggy Chandler. She had a seventy-nine. Peggy Chandler was one of the big favorites. She'd finished one-two in this championship for three straight years.

After the qualifying round the top thirty-two of us went into the match play. My first opponent was Mrs. James Hutchinson of Houston. I beat her, six up and five to play. The newspaper accounts of the opening round said that my long tee shots were one of the big features of the day, but they also said that I would face the "most severe golf test" of my career in the second round, when I had to play Mrs. Walter Woodul of Houston.

Maybe that helped to get me "up" for Mrs. Woodul. Or maybe she just had a bad day. Anyhow, I won out by eight-and-six. It was my easiest win of the tournament. In reporting on that match the papers said, "Miss Didrikson has yet to leave the first tee without a big gallery trailing."

There was a driving contest that same day, and I hit the longest one—250 yards. After the contest was over the people yelled for me to hit a few more, so I did. I got one ball out there 265 yards.

Now I was in the quarterfinals. There I faced Mrs. F. C. Rochon from Wichita Falls. Women's par at River Oaks was seventy-seven. I was two over par on the first nine holes, but I played even par coming back. I took the match by three-and-two.

That was a pretty tough battle, but things were due to get tougher. I found that out in the semifinals the next day against Mrs. R. E. Winger of Fort Worth. It was a gloomy, windy day, with some showers mixed in. After the first nine holes I was two up. Then the rain got so bad, and the course got so messy, that we had to stop playing.

We waited and waited for the weather to ease up. It was several hours before things improved enough for us to go back out there and start playing again. We picked up where we'd left off—at the tenth hole. When we got on the green, it was so waterlogged that I thought I'd try chipping my ball into the cup instead of using my putter. The shot didn't work. Mrs. Winger got down all right with her putter to win the hole, so my lead was cut to one up.

I played her even through the next four holes, then she

won the fifteenth to square the match. We halved the next two, and went into the last hole with the match still tied.

My drive was long, but it went off the fairway into some trees at the right. Mrs. Winger's drive was right down the middle but not quite as far. She caught a trap with her second shot, while I got back on the fairway with mine. Then we both hit the green with our third shots. My ball was about twenty feet from the cup. Hers was about three feet farther away.

It had stopped raining, but that green still was plenty wet. Mrs. Winger took her putt, and it was a beauty. The ball stopped just at the edge of the hole. Then I made my putt. It was an uphill roll. Water was coming off that ball as it started up there. It kept on going, and it rolled right in the cup.

"Some women cried over the dramatic finish," Bill Parker wrote in his Associated Press story about the match. "Men hollered. Babe smiled, walked off the green—still America's wonder girl athlete and probably the most promising woman golf player in the United States." He wound up by saying that I would be the underdog in the finals the next day, since it was only my second tournament and I'd be going up against a real experienced player.

That was Peggy Chandler, who had won the qualifying medal and was one of the original tournament favorites. This was the fourth year in a row she'd reached the finals. She'd taken the championship one of the other three times.

The final was a thirty-six-hole match. It was still overcast when we set out on our first eighteen-hole round in the morning. The course was soggy. There were a lot of water puddles around. In spite of all the wetness, I started off as if I was going to set that course on fire. On the first hole I got an eagle three, while she took a six.

We seesawed back and forth for several holes after that, and then I hit a real hot streak. There was a gallery of several thousand people, and most of them seemed to be yelling for me. For a while there I gave them plenty to yell about. Inside of twelve holes I was five up.

Then I lost the touch, and Peggy Chandler got hot. She won all those holes back. In fact, she took every one of the last six holes in the morning round, so when we went in for lunch she was one up.

People told me after that everybody was saying, "It's the old story. A kid against a veteran. The kid has folded. She's all through now."

By the time of the afternoon round there was bright sunshine. The fairways were pretty well dried out now, although there was still water in some of the hazards. The weather had settled down, and I began to settle down too. I was still hitting some wild shots, especially with my irons. All day long I kept getting myself in trouble, and having to recover from it. Only now I was bringing the recoveries off. I'd been seven over par in the morning. In the afternoon I shot an even-par round.

But Peggy Chandler was shooting good golf herself. I birdied the first hole in the afternoon. She birdied it too. It kept on like that. She was matching me stroke for stroke, and sometimes going me one stroke better.

It was the eighth hole that gave me back my confidence. She was three up then. I hadn't won a hole all afternoon, but on the eighth green I dropped a twenty-five-foot putt for a birdie four to beat out her par five.

94

I won the next hole, too. She took the one after that. Then I won two holes in a row to even up the match. It stayed that way coming into the sixteenth hole, which was the thirty-fourth hole of our match.

The sixteenth was a long hole—a par five. Peggy Chandler hit a good tee shot. Mine was even better. It went 250 yards, way in front of hers, only it landed in a ditch that ran across the middle of the fairway.

She played her second shot not too far short of the green. Then I took my three iron and banged my ball out of that ditch and on past the green. It came to a stop about twenty yards beyond in a roadway that the trucks used. It wound up in a big rut—almost a small ditch. There was water in the bottom of it.

Peggy Chandler was farther away from the pin than I was, so her third shot came next. She hit the ball up there so close to the cup that she had almost a sure birdie four.

That really put the pressure on me for my third shot. I couldn't afford to lose this hole. I couldn't afford to lose any holes at all if I was going to win this golf championship.

I studied that shot carefully. It was a tough one for a beginner. The water in this deep rut covered the lower part of my ball. I said to myself, "Now Babe, you can't make any more mistakes. You've got to take your time and play this one just right."

I took a sand wedge that Gene Sarazen had given me when I first met him a while before. I thought of everything I'd been taught about how to play this kind of shot—how I should stand with my weight on my left foot and all that. And I remembered the first rule of golf that everybody had told me: "Look at the ball real good."

So I swung, and I did everything right, and dug that ball up there. I could see it running toward the pin. And then there was a roar, and the people behind me came rushing up, and somebody knocked me face down into that muddy ditch. The ball had gone into the hole for an eagle three.

That turned out to be the deciding shot of the match. It put me one up with only two holes to play. We halved the thirty-fifth. On the last hole, which was a par five, I was on the green in two shots, while it took her three. When I putted to the edge of the cup with my third shot, and she failed to hole out her putt for a four, she conceded me a birdie four and the match. So I won it two up.

I was on top of the world that day. It had taken me longer than I originally figured to get going in golf, but I was rolling at last. I had the Texas championship, and now I was ready to shoot for the national championship. I wanted to hit all the big women's tournaments around the country. I already had my entry in for the Southern Women's Amateur at Louisville on May twentieth.

Well, I had won that Texas tournament on April twenty-seventh. Two days later the newspapers reported that the United States Golf Association was looking into my case to see whether I should be allowed to play in any more amateur tournaments. It seemed they'd had complaints from people who thought that because I'd done professional things in athletics, I didn't belong in amateur golf.

On May fourteenth the bottom dropped out of everything. The USGA said I couldn't play in the Southern or any of the other tournaments. They ruled me out of women's golf on the grounds that I was a professional.

96

CHAPTER 8

When the United States Golf Association declared me ineligible for the women's amateur golf tournaments back there in the spring of 1935, they never did announce the reasons why they had decided I was a pro. I know that complaints by certain Texas women entered into it. Anyhow, Archie M. Reid of the USGA was the fellow who issued the ruling, and all he said for publication was that they were doing it "for the best interest of the game."

A lot of people in Texas got up in arms. Ben S. Woodhead, president of the Beaumont Country Club, petitioned the USGA to give me a full hearing. I had represented the club in the Texas women's championship, and he said they were confident I could clear myself of any charges.

Jack Burke called it "the dirtiest deal I've heard of in a long time." Jimmy Demaret said it was "the biggest joke of the year." A lot of the sportswriters panned the decision. The Texas Women's Golf Association spoke up in my behalf too.

I didn't do any sounding off myself. When you get a big setback like that, there's no use crying about it. It was something like the time in 1953 when I found out I had cancer. You just have to face your problem and figure out what to do next.

What I did back there in 1935 was to sign a contract with a sporting-goods company, P. Goldsmith Sons. Later they merged with the MacGregor Golf Company, and that became the brand name for their golf equipment. Goldsmith paid me a retainer of $2500 a year and brought out a line of women's golf clubs in my name, just as if I was already Bobby Jones or something. And I got booked for a series of exhibition matches with Gene Sarazen, who was the top man in the business at that time.

Gene played the golf and I put on the show. We'd go around to these different places and team up against some other pair. Our first opponents were Helen Hicks, who was one of the first women golf champions to turn professional, and Johnny Rogers. I believe the match was played at George S. May's Tam o' Shanter Country Club in Niles, Illinois. The grass off the fairway was real high, and I could hardly move around in it. I was all dressed up for my first professional appearance. There were no special sports clothes for women to play golf in then—no golf dresses or golf shoes.

Sometimes both of our opponents would be men pros. These were best-ball matches, and Gene Sarazen carried the load. I generally didn't help him much, except maybe for

98

I'd had several boy friends as a youngster, but when I met George Zaharias at the '38 Los Angeles Open, I knew this was IT Less than a year later we were married in St. Louis.

Winning the 1940 Western Open, at Milwaukee, was a big step. Mrs C. B Willard (*left*) head of the Western, presented the cup filled with white orchids as Mrs Russell Mann, runner-up, and a grand sport, looks on

Just before teeing off in a War Relief match with John Montague, Sylvia Annenberg and Babe Ruth We drove off at 1 P.M with nearly 25,000 in our wake I recall I had a six-footer for a 32 on the 9th hole when the mob swallowed us up

I'd never driven a trotter before when the chance came at Pine-hurst in '43 It was exhilarating to say the least.

Eleanor Tennant, who coached Alice Marble to two world titles, took me in hand in '44, and I was really enthusiastic—until the USLTA banned me as a pro in a sport I'd never even competed in.

Way back when, I struggled with sand traps but after being on an exhibition tour with Gene Sarazen, sand and I were friends

This was taken on the practice green at Augusta, Georgia, in April '47 I had decided to try for the British Women's Amateur .. and Bob Jones was checking my stroke

Battling the elements At Gullane, in those British Isles, weather is a tremendous factor. Here, I'm driving from the 3rd tee in the 2nd round

My 3rd-round foe, Mrs. Val Reddan, former Irish champion, was a lovely girl but wasn't on her game the day we met. I took it 6-and-4

Wide World Photo

I like this picture, taken from the rough on the 8th hole at Gullane
I recovered poorly from practically this identical spot in the morning
round of my final match against Jacqueline Gordon, but in the afternoon
I whipped that ball up and out.. for a long carry, stiff to the pin
Jacqueline, wearing checkered skirt, watches flight of the ball I won
it 5-and-4

Sport and General Press Agency, Limited

The British liked me, I hope, almost as much as I loved them Here,
I'm receiving the big cup, the first American-born girl to bring it home.

Denver Home-coming It was the red carpet when
George took me home following the British victory.

When the movie people offered me $300,000 to make a series of instructional shorts, I couldn't reject the offer. I turned pro again under the managerial eyes of Fred Corcoran P S Those golf movies never jelled nor did the $300,000.

Renewing friendship with another swatter Ted Williams, a big stakes winner in Fred Corcoran's promotional stable, can blast a golf ball too, but after talking things over we decided Ted would stick to his game, me to mine

This time I signed up with the Wilson Sporting
Goods people This is a lovely study of L. B. Icely
—and what a promoter!—Wilson's president, who
died early in '48

I received expert coaching from these star bait casters at the Sportsmen's Show in Boston Jack Sharkey points; Ted Williams views all quizzically as I register a frozen stare

At the Los Angeles Celebrity Tournament, Danny Kaye shows why he hasn't been tapped for the love scene in Romeo and Juliet.

I put on a trick-shot exhibition at the Yankee Stadium before a night game when the old baseball yen returned I pitched to Joe DiMaggio, a gentleman, and batted against Spec Shea, another gallant. It was fun!

International News Photo

Wide World Photo

George May pins a competitor's number on Joe Louis As an amateur, Joe often moves around in the 70's

With Jim Thorpe at the Celebrity Tournament at Washington We had been voted the top athletes of the first half-century

Wide World Photo

Scouts Jimmy Dolvin and Cecil Cannon, two boy friends at Druid Hills, Atlanta in 1951. This was during the Women's Golf Open

When you're banging at Colonel Par every day, those 1-putt greens are money in the till. Here, my bid for a bird just misses in that '51 Women's Open. Betsy Rawls won the title with a crackling 293

Body English sometimes helps that ball to drop When the chips are down, this is strictly involuntary action!

I wish he was mine . and I guess I show it. With my caddy, Kent Foley, 16, after winning the Western Open in 1950. A sweetheart, young Kent earned the $100 I gave him

Dot Kielty, Women's Amateur winner, Frank Stranahan, Men's Amateur titlist and me with Women's Pro cup at Tam O'Shanter in 1950 My total of 293 for 72 holes was 11 under women's par I was in a wonderful streak

We were playing at Ponte Vedra, Florida, when a press poll announced I'd been selected as the girl athlete of the year with the Bauer sisters, Marlene and Alice, in 3rd place. They're from Midland, Texas and they're sure cute.

Wilson Sportex

You know, sometimes our caddies must think our golf
bags are all this size! But really, they're not.

The movie colony takes its golf seriously and
Katharine Hepburn has a pretty fine golfing
background. She once reached the high brackets
of women's play in Connecticut, her home state.

Spencer Tracy, a sports promoter in the movie, "Pat
and Mike," with (L to R) Helen Dettweiler, Bev Hanson, me and Betty Hicks. This was taken on the Coast
in April '52, shortly before I became really ill

one or two holes. I wasn't a finished golfer yet. But I could give the gallery some laughs, and I could hit that long ball off the tee.

Sometimes the headline on the local sports page wouldn't even mention who won the match. It would be, DIDRIKSON PANICS 'EM AT BEVERLY, or, BABE DIDRIKSON OUT-DRIVES GENE SARAZEN.

It wasn't too unusual for me to get tee shots of 280 yards, 300 yards and more. Once I hit a drive 346 yards with the benefit of the wind and a good hard bounce. The other women didn't slug the ball that way. Take Joyce Wethered, the British star. She was one of the women golfers I used to read about when I was a kid growing up. At the time of my Sarazen tour she had gone professional and was making appearances in this country. I got to play against her a couple of times.

She had a beautiful swing. She'd been classed by quite a few experts as the finest swinger in the game, man or woman. And that was the way of golf over in England and Scotland. You didn't hit the ball. You swung at it. The idea was to develop a nice, graceful swing.

But Joyce Wethered didn't hit the ball very far. I think I could have taken a two-iron and driven it past where she hit her wood. I don't mean that she wasn't a great all-around player. She and I scored about the same in those two matches. But in women's golf today you've got to have that distance. You've got to be a slugger as well as a swinger. You don't just go for the green. You go for the pin.

It was on that tour with Gene Sarazen that I got my start at entertaining galleries. I'd kid him, and kid the crowd, and of course he'd kid me some too. Maybe I'd overdrive a green, and mess myself up coming back, and he'd say, "Too bad."

I'd say, "Too bad? What's too bad? Didn't you see that drive?"

Or I'd get into a bad spot, and turn around to the gallery before I swung and say, "Watch this. My best shot of the day." And darned if I generally didn't bring it off.

I just love a gallery. It bothers some athletes to have people always crowding around them. I wouldn't feel right if the people weren't there. Even in a tournament, I like to kid around with the gallery, except when I'm real tired, the way I sometimes get if I overdo things.

And when I'm putting on a golf demonstration—we call them clinics—I'll break my neck to give the people a good show. I'll bear down on that old Texas drawl, because they seem to like it, and I'll say, "You all come closer now, because you've heard of Walter Hagen, you've heard of Bobby Jones, you've heard of Ben Hogan, but today you're looking at the best."

I have an assortment of trick shots I've worked out to loosen up the audience. I'll set up five balls on the tee, and drive them one after another, and the fifth ball must be in the air before the first one has landed. Or I'll shoot left-handed—I can hit a ball pretty good that way too.

On the green I may stick my foot in front of the ball, and make the ball hop over it into the cup. Then I'll throw down some clubs, like an ice skater setting up a row of barrels to leap across, and I'll hit the ball with my putter so that it jumps over all the clubs.

I keep wisecracking with the gallery. I may hit a real long one, and then say, "Boy! Don't you men wish you could hit a ball like that?" I always tell them, "Ladies and gentlemen, whatever I say today can't be held against me, because it's for your entertainment." And I've never had a gallery that didn't seem to take my kidding the way it was intended.

Gene Sarazen and I drew fine galleries during our tour. We played these exhibition matches at country clubs all over the East and the Middle West. He was just as wonderful to me as he could be. I kept asking him questions and questions. If I was going to be the best, I wanted to learn from the best. And he was the best in championship golf at that time.

In between matches he would get out and work with me. He was a master of trap shots, and he's the one who really taught me how to play out of traps. I guess I'm now considered one of the best trap-shot players in golf myself, and that's been a strong point in my game. I seldom get into a spot so bad that I'm not capable of playing a good shot out.

Once when we had two weeks off between exhibitions, Gene said, "Babe, I talked to my wife Mary on the phone last night, and she wants you to come visit us during this layoff. You can rest a while, and then we'll work on the golf some more."

So I went to visit the Sarazens. They had this beautiful farm in Connecticut. There were a lot of cows and stuff—it was a dairy farm. They had a little pond with nice cool spring water. I rested and swam and practiced golf.

I came off that Sarazen tour at the end of the summer in 1935 with a really good bankroll. I'd played something like eighteen of those exhibition matches around the East and Middle West at $500 each. I was still getting my $2500 a

101

year from the sporting-goods company, and they were giving me all the golf supplies I needed free. Now I was set to go out to Southern California and concentrate on my golf game for a good long while, the way I'd tried to do a couple of years before.

I took Momma and Poppa with me, and also my sister Lillie and my younger brother Arthur, or Bubba. I'd bought Poppa a car after his operation in 1933, when I began making money again on the basketball stuff. I got him a 1933 De Soto sedan. I believe it helped make him well again. He was so happy with it. For the first time in their lives he and Momma could go riding around wherever they wanted. He'd be out in the garage every chance he got, polishing up the car as he puffed away on his pipe.

I had my own car, so we drove out to California in the two automobiles. We got a nice little apartment with two bedrooms and a fold-down bed in the living room. I think the rent was about $27 a month, and we watched our other expenses too. But we were enjoying life.

Nowadays I sometimes have trouble sleeping, but then I could really sleep. I'd be pounding my ear in the morning, and Momma would wake me up. She'd have breakfast ready for me, and then she'd say, "Now go play your golf."

I took some more lessons from Stan Kertes, and I kept on practicing and practicing. There was one driving range where I'd often hit balls from morning to night. Some nights the proprietor would keep the lights on an hour or two after his regular closing time, because I was giving a show that was good for his business. There'd be a big crowd of people standing around watching me.

For the next couple of years I spent most of my time on

the West Coast, working on my golf and playing exhibitions. The Goldsmith people booked some for me, and I made appearances around California with Stan Kertes, and things like that.

Some writers have said that around this time a big change took place in me. Their idea is that I used to be all tomboy, with none of the usual girls' interests, and then all of a sudden I switched over to being feminine.

Well, with almost any woman athlete, you seem to get that tomboy talk. It happens especially with girls who play things that generally aren't considered women's sports, like basketball and baseball, the way I did.

I hear the same routine about girls on the golf circuit today. They call young Mary Lena Faulk "the tomboy from Thomasville, Georgia." The only reason for it is that "tomboy" goes with "Thomasville." There's no more tomboy to Mary Lena Faulk than any girl you ever saw. She's as much interested in dancing and things like that as anybody else. All the girls are.

Patty Berg has been "The Redheaded Tomboy" and "The Minneapolis Tomboy." There've been stories about how she used to play tackle football with the boys in the neighborhood where she grew up. One of the boys was Bud Wilkinson, who is the University of Oklahoma football coach today. I met a fellow once who said, "I played football with Patty Berg, and she tackled me and broke my shoulder blade."

Actually, a lot of writers just have to sit at a typewriter, and they don't always know the athlete or personality they're writing about. Sometimes they get to meet them and sometimes they don't.

As for me, I was determined to be an athlete, and a fine

103

athlete. But I was always interested in the women's things around the house, like cooking and sewing and decorating. I loved all the pretty things, and I still love all the pretty things.

I often have people come up to me and say, "I have a daughter who's going to be a wonderful athlete. She's the biggest tomboy in the neighborhood." And I think that's fine, being a tomboy when you're a youngster. Because the years will take care of any girl who is a tomboy. When you get to a certain age, and you start growing in places where you weren't developed before, then nothing can stop you from changing. You've just got to go with it.

But I don't believe my personality has changed. I think anyone who knew me when I was a kid will tell you that I'm still the same Babe. It's just that as you get older, you're not as rambunctious as you used to be. You mellow down a little bit.

I had dates and boyfriends from the time when I was working in Dallas. For a while there were two that were fighting each other. I couldn't help getting a kick out of that. I went with one of them for several years. He was serious about wanting to get married, but I wasn't. I was too busy working on my sports career.

I still wasn't thinking about marriage when I entered the Los Angeles Open tournament in January 1938. I was twenty-three then. The Los Angeles Open is one of the regular tournaments on the men's circuit, but there was no rule that said a woman couldn't play in it. So I got in there. I knew I wasn't going to beat the top men pros, but I was still trying to establish myself as the greatest woman golfer.

You didn't have to qualify for the tournament, although

only the leading scorers for the first thirty-six holes were allowed to play the last thirty-six. I wasn't the only one who didn't have any business being in it. There were some fellows who were good part-time golfers, but not in a class with the real pros. One was C. Pardee Erdman, a Presbyterian minister who was professor of religion at Occidental College in Los Angeles—he's dean of the college now.

Another was George Zaharias, a big-time professional wrestler. I found out afterwards that he'd done some of his golf playing with Lloyd Mangrum and a couple of other pros. One day when he broke eighty he said as a joke, "Now I'm ready to enter the Los Angeles Open." And they told him, "Why not? You'll have some fun and it'll be good experience for you."

Well, they had the three of us play together—the girl, the minister and the wrestler. One of the Los Angeles sportswriters—I think it was Mel Gallagher—said, "Babe, come on over here and meet your partners. I want our photographer to get a picture of the three of you."

What an introduction George and I had! One minute we were saying hello, and the next minute photographers were crowding around and calling for him to put wrestling holds on me. He put his arm around me, pretending to apply neck holds and stuff. And I didn't mind it at all.

We drove off the first tee. As I walked down the fairway I kept looking back at George, and he seemed to be sort of watching me.

George was twenty-nine years old then. He was husky and black-haired and handsome. His parents were Greek. The sportswriters called him "The Crying Greek from Cripple Creek," which was a Colorado town, but George actually came from Pueblo in Colorado. He was born Theodore Veto-yanis. He changed his name to George Zaharias after he went into the ring—the promoters thought his original name wasn't catchy enough.

George's dad went to work in a steel mill in Colorado after coming to this country, and then settled down on a farm outside Pueblo. These are all things I learned later on, of course. George worked on his father's farm, and also in the steel mills, which must have helped to develop those tremendous muscles of his. When he was still in his teens he went to live with an uncle in Oklahoma City and learn the hat-cleaning business. He shined shoes too.

Then the wrestling bug bit him. He had a hard time breaking in, but finally he became a real attraction. By the time I met him, he'd already been able to build a new home for his parents, and set a couple of brothers-in-law up in business, and pay for the education of his two younger brothers, Chris and Tom. People paid to see George wrestle because in the ring he was the big bad villain that everybody hated, but outside it he had the nicest quiet-spoken way.

A lot of great golf was played the first day of that 1938 Los Angeles Open. Jimmy Thomson and Willie Goggin had sixty-fives. Lloyd Mangrum, Henry Picard, and a half a dozen others had sixty-eights.

But practically all the gallery went with George Zaharias, Pardee Erdman and myself. Those people didn't see too much good golf. My mind didn't seem to be on my game. Pardee Erdman, who is one of the finest fellows I know, was the only one of us to do any real playing.

I liked the way a writer named Jack Singer summed it

all up in one of the Los Angeles newspapers the next day. He wrote:

"The only person in the whole gallery who was certain of what was going on was Mrs. Edgar Richards. Now there's one woman who knows what the score is. She ought to. She was the scorekeeper. I guess religion still pays, because the professor finished with a 75. Zaharias finished with 83, the Babe finished with 84 and Mrs. Richards finished with writer's cramp."

After our round was over George invited us to have refreshments with him and some of the other boys, so we did. Pardee Erdman and I had cokes—the others had cold beer. We sat around quite a while talking, and then I had to excuse myself and get back home. Momma and Lillie were with me at the time, and I knew they'd be waiting dinner and everything. Poppa was back home in Beaumont, working and looking after things there.

As I left, George called out, "I'll be seeing you tomorrow."

With my eighty-four in the first round, there was no chance that I'd qualify for the final thirty-six holes—which I did do a few years later in the Los Angeles Open—but I was looking forward to that second round. I already had the feeling that this George Zaharias was my kind of guy, and it turned out that he was thinking I was his kind of girl.

The second day we sat down for refreshments again after playing our golf, and George invited me to come back to the apartment where he was living with his brothers, Tom and Chris, and have dinner with them. I phoned home and told them I was going out for dinner.

Each of us had our own car there at the Griffith Park course, so we set off in the two cars. I was supposed to be following George. But this was strange territory for me. I was living over in Hollywood, right near the Paramount studio, while George was in another section. I got confused in the traffic and took a left turn that I wasn't supposed to make.

In his mirror George saw me take that wrong fork. He got his own car turned around. He came after me and finally caught up to me. He said, "Are you trying to run away from me?"

But I wasn't trying to do that. We got to his apartment, and George broiled some steaks. I met his brothers, who were wrestlers too. Pretty soon they were demonstrating holds on me. George was watching pretty close to see that they didn't get rough with me. Which they didn't, of course.

Those steaks were fine. I remember another night when George cooked dinner for me. He put a chicken in the oven, and pretty soon it started to smell bad. The smell got worse and worse. George took the chicken out to see what was wrong. He found that they'd cleaned the chicken at the store, and then wrapped the insides in a little package and put it in the chicken. George had been roasting the insides and all.

After that first dinner at George's apartment we made a date to meet at the golf course the next day and watch the boys play the third round of the Los Angeles Open. George and I had been eliminated by then. We watched some of the third round, and he asked me if I'd like to go out dancing that night.

I said, "Sure. I love to dance."

I went home first. George came there to pick me up, and met Momma and Lillie. Momma liked him straight off.

108

We went dancing at a place called the Cotton Club. It's gone now. I remember we each had our pictures sketched in charcoal. He autographed his and gave it to me, and I autographed mine and gave it to him.

It was about one o'clock when I got home. Momma wasn't used to that, because I'd always been a great one for training and getting to bed early. She was waiting up, and she said, "Babe, you're out late. I was worried about you."

I said, "Oh, Momma, it's all right. George and I wanted to do some dancing."

She said, "Well, that's fine. He's a nice man."

It sort of built up from there. George took to calling me "Romance," and when I wrote a note to him I'd sign it "Romance." We were going together real steady, except that he had to be away a lot to wrestle, and I had my golf bookings.

I might stop by his place and find nobody home, and slide a note under his door: "I was here, but you weren't. Romance." Then when he got back my telephone would ring, and I'd say, "Hello," and he'd say, "This is Romance."

Finally the time came when I was going to drive Momma and Lillie home to Beaumont. George had to stay and wrestle around California. We said we'd write and keep in touch by telephone, and see each other again as soon as we could.

Momma and Lillie and I set off in the car. We were going to stop off and visit my oldest sister, Dora, who had married and gone to live in Phoenix, Arizona. She's still living in Arizona, although she's in a place called Morristown now. Her married name is Mrs. Clarence F. Cole. Dora has two sons, Frank and Harold.

The farther away we got from California, the worse I

was feeling. Momma could sense it. I'd been telling her how crazy I was about George, and she thought it was fine that we were in love with each other.

When we got to Phoenix, she said, "You want to go back to California, don't you?"

I said, "Yes, Momma, I do. Would you and Lillie mind taking the train the rest of the way to Beaumont?"

She said, "Yes, we'll take the train. You go on back and see George."

I drove that car as fast as I could go 420 miles back to George's apartment. And he wasn't there. I found a note on the door. It said, "Romance, I'm in San Francisco." He'd gone up there to keep a wrestling date.

The way George told it later was, "I knew one of us had to come back, and in case it was you, I wanted you to know where I was."

So George wasn't home at the apartment, but his brother Chris was. I said, "Chris, will you drive up to San Francisco with me to see George?"

He said, "You mean now? Do you know how long a drive that is? It's almost 460 miles." Then he said, "All right. I'll take you."

We drove all night. Not long after dawn we got to the St. Marks Hotel in San Francisco, where the wrestlers were staying. Chris and I went up and pounded on the door of George's room. He came out and said, "Come here, Romance." He gave me a big kiss. And then I wasn't lonesome anymore.

I got a room at the St. Marks myself so I could be near George until he finished up with his wrestling in San Francisco. Eventually I did have to go to Beaumont, but from then on, George tried to arrange his bookings so he'd be near where I was, and I did the same thing with my golf appearances.

We got to see a lot of each other around the time of the Western Women's Open in June. The tournament was held that year in Colorado Springs, which wasn't far from George's hometown of Pueblo. He fixed up his wrestling dates for around there. He took me out to meet his folks, and I spent quite a bit of time with them. His mother didn't speak too much English, but she and I got along fine just the same.

I was eliminated in the semifinal round of the tournament. But that particular summer, losing a golf match didn't seem to matter as much to me as it ordinarily did.

From Colorado we drove in my car to St. Louis. I left George there and went on to Cincinnati, where my sporting-goods company had its headquarters. Then I came back to St. Louis myself.

We announced our engagement in St. Louis on July 22, 1938. We wanted to have a wedding with both the families present and everything. George was mostly wrestling out of St. Louis at this point, and I was able to spend a lot of my time there too. But one or the other of us kept having to take off for an appearance some place else. What with this commitment and that, we never could seem to work out a date for the wedding.

Finally it was December. We were both in St. Louis again, and George got real stern with me. He said, "We're going to get married this week or call the deal off."

I said, "It's a deal. Let's go!"

CHAPTER **9**

When George and I decided not to go through any more delays on getting married, Tom Packs, the St. Louis wrestling promoter, volunteered to hold the wedding at his house. So we arranged to get married there on December 23, 1938. It was a very nice affair. We invited some of our best St. Louis friends, like Leo Durocher and Joe Medwick of the Cardinals, and their wives.

Then there was Bud Hobart, and Morris Shevlin, and Mr. and Mrs. Sidney Solomon and Mr. and Mrs. Matt Zottka. The ceremony was performed by another friend, Justice of the Peace A. P. Jannopoula.

Leo Durocher was George's best man, while Mrs. Durocher stood up with me. That was Leo's former wife. She was a dress designer there in St. Louis. She made me a beautiful outfit for the wedding.

When the ceremony was all over, I just sat back in a chair and let out a great big sigh. George said, "Well, honey, do you feel any different now?"

I said, "Yeah."

Then he said, "Honey, I've got you at last."

And I said, "No, I've got you."

Do you remember the song, "A Slow Boat To China," that was popular around then? Well, George asked me where I'd like to go for my honeymoon trip, and I said, "I think I'd like to take a slow boat to Australia."

But there couldn't be any honeymoon trip just then. We both had too many business dates to keep. We stayed around St. Louis for a while, and then we went back to the West Coast. We were living near our friends Bill and Betty Bryant, who were operating the Brentwood Country Club.

One morning in April of 1939, George suddenly says out of a clear sky, "Honey, get yourself packed up. We're going on a trip."

I said, "Where are we going? Is it to Florida?"

He said, "I'm not going to tell you. Just get enough clothes together so you'll be ready for warm weather or cool."

Bill Bryant came by in his station wagon, and we loaded our stuff in. He drove us to a pier in San Pedro, and George took me aboard this boat. I said to George, "Now will you tell me? Where are we going?"

He said, "Honey, we're on that slow boat to Australia."

On the way over we stopped off at Honolulu for three weeks. We rented a place where we could keep house. We loafed around the beach, and I tried out recipes for Hawaiian dishes and everything. And I rented a sewing machine and ran up half a dozen Hawaiian-style shirts for George, with those short sleeves and the fancy patterns.

Then we got on a boat to sail the rest of the way to Australia. We were traveling first class, and it was like a morgue —dressing for dinner every night, and nobody having any fun. There was no action.

The people down in third class seemed to be enjoying themselves. So we asked the purser to switch us to a third-class cabin. It wasn't as big or comfortable as our first-class cabin, but we figured we'd have a better time that way. And we were right.

We met a swell gang of people in third class. There was a whole troupe of entertainers going over to perform in Australia. We became very good friends with some of them, like Tony La Mont and his wife Betty. She sang, and he walked the tightrope and did comedy stuff. There were tumblers and acrobats. And there were the Andrini Brothers, who played the mandolin and guitar.

We'd get out on the top deck at night, with the water as beautiful as anything in the moonlight. The Andrini brothers would play, and some of the other musicians. And the singers would cut loose, and I'd get in there with my harmonica. It was a wonderful trip.

I was just enjoying life in those months after I got married. I was putting on a lot of weight and not bearing down very hard on my golf. But I found myself back in the golf business when we got to Australia. That George, with his business head, didn't see why we shouldn't make some money out of our trip. All during that time when I thought he'd

114

forgotten about my wanting to go to Australia, he'd been working out arrangements. He'd lined up some wrestling matches for himself, and a lot of golf exhibitions for me.

A fellow named Archie Keene, who had promoted an Australian tour for Gene Sarazen and Helen Hicks, made my bookings. They gave us a little bitty English car to travel around in. You should have seen George trying to get into it. One of the cartoonists over there did a cartoon of us stuck in the mud, with George sitting in the car and me at the back end pushing it out.

I played all around Australia—Sydney, Perth, Bath and dozens of other places. About the only big place I didn't get to play in was Melbourne. Every time I was scheduled there it rained.

In one exhibition I had the Prime Minister of Australia in my gallery. I don't remember his name. He was a man about eighty years old, and he walked around the whole eighteen holes. At the finish, he said he'd enjoyed watching and would like to see me play again some time.

When I first got over there, some people didn't believe all the talk they'd heard about my long hitting and so forth. This story by an Australian golf writer named Jack Dillo shows the way things were:

"The golf of Miss Didrikson has made a very great impression on Victorian golfers. Upon her arrival I advised her that her advance publicity had been of a silly ballyhoo variety, and that the intelligent people who supported golf were skeptical about the tales of her long drives.

"This really delightful girl accepted the challenge squarely. The following day at Victoria in a private exhibition for a handful of writers, what this magnificent specimen of athletic womanhood showed us certainly was impressive.

"The plain fact is that Miss Didrikson is a vastly better golfer than Miss Helen Hicks, Miss Pam Barton or any other woman we have seen. She can hit a ball farther than all except a very few men. At Victoria the day was bitterly cold, the turf was thick and dead, and generally it was a perfect day for a test for anyone to endure. Here are some of the genuine and checked figures, with turf not helping the least and over level ground. She hit drives of 230, 245 and 250 yards in the first three holes. She hit her first mashie 170 yards and another 180 yards. In bunkers her class was that of Sarazen. Her approach work from 140–30 yards from the green was not completely finished and she was good but not overly impressive on the greens. If Miss Didrikson tightens up her short game, she may get a place among the best men professionals in golf."

I played big courses in Australia and I played little ones. Once George and I drove 125 miles in our little car to get to a nine-hole course in the back country. When we arrived, I wondered at first why we'd bothered to come. The course was in terrible shape. They didn't have the water to keep it up. There were cracks in the greens and everything.

The clubhouse looked like an old barn that hadn't been used for months. There were cobwebs all over the place. When I got there, eight or ten women were in this clubhouse rushing around like fury. I didn't know what they were trying to do.

Outside I saw a surrey here, and a horse and buggy there. It turned out that one family had driven their horse 120 miles to get to this exhibition. Another had come eighty miles. There were people from all sorts of out-of-the-way spots who couldn't have got to see me play anywhere except at this little club. The course had been closed down, but they opened it up for my exhibition. They cut the grass on the greens and all that.

I played around the course, and then they invited me to come into the clubhouse. I couldn't believe it was the same old barn I'd seen earlier. Those women had gotten it all cleaned and spruced up. They had ribbons strung up top to take away the rafter effect. There were decorations all around. And they had these big long tables set with beautiful table cloths, and just loaded down with cakes and cookies and tea. I received a lot of fine hospitality and entertainment while I was in Australia, but that day sticks in my mind more than any of the others, because it was so unexpected and they'd gone to so much trouble over it.

One of my biggest golfing events over there was a special exhibition I had with the Australian PGA champion, Charley Conners. We played at a beautiful course, the Yarra Yarra Country Club. It was a rainy day, but there was a big crowd of people out with their umbrellas and rubber boots and rain-coats.

They didn't seem to have the arrangements for handling a crowd that we do at the big courses in this country. Over here they put ropes up to try to keep the people off the fairways and stuff. At Yarra Yarra, there was little or none of that. We'd hit our drives and start walking down the fairway. I'd look back, and the fairway behind us would be just black with people following after us. That crowd almost ruined their lovely grass.

I played with Charley Conners under men's conditions, driving from the back tees and everything. I was shooting good golf in spite of the weather. Playing my second shot on the last hole, which was a par five, I hit the best four-iron of my life. The ball sailed high over a clump of trees and went on the green right up to the pin.

So I closed out with an eagle three. That gave me a seventy-two for the round. Charley Conners shot a seventy-one. This was the performance that did most to convince them in Australia that I could play golf. I'd come within one stroke of tying their men's professional champion.

Our Australian friends gave us a wonderful sendoff at the boat when we finally started home after several months. We made a side trip to New Zealand, where I gave an exhibition at Aukland, and then sailed on to Honolulu. We had another stopover there. When we came off the boat, I headed almost immediately for a golf course, to limber up my golf muscles. I went around the eighteen holes in sixty-eight strokes.

I'd taken off all my extra weight by now, and got my game sharpened up again. George did some wrestling in Hawaii, and I played some golf. It was mostly practicing. I got to play rounds with Harry Cooper and some other pros. And George and I were on the beach a lot with friends like Dan Topping. We learned surfboard riding and things like that.

There was one golf exhibition I had with a Hawaiian boy and girl who were considered very promising youngsters. I don't know the name of the boy, and until recently, I'd forgotten who the girl was. She was small and lean. She couldn't have weighed as much as 120 pounds.

Then a little while back Mrs. Jackie Pung joined our women's professional golf tour, after winning the National

Women's Amateur championship. She said, "Do you remember me playing against you when you came through Hawaii back in 1939?" She showed me pictures of herself at that age, and sure enough, it was the same little girl. I'd never have recognized her, because Jackie weighed 220 or 230 pounds at the time she went on our professional circuit.

We got back home to California in the fall of 1939. And George began to do some heavy thinking about my golf future. It was something that had worried me, too. Here I'd been practicing all the time, and developed this fine golf game, and about all I could do with it was play exhibition matches. I wasn't getting a chance to show whether I was the best woman player, because I was barred from practically all the women's tournaments as a professional.

At the time when they'd declared me a professional in the spring of 1935, there was only one tournament of any importance that I could enter. That was the Western Women's Open. Then my friend Bertha Bowen, of Fort Worth, helped get a Texas Women's Open going, which made two.

But two a year isn't enough to give you tournament sharpness. And those tournaments were match play, which I've never thought was as fair a test as medal play. In medal play, everybody just plays the course, and the one with the lowest total score wins. In match play, anybody is apt to get a hot round and knock out anybody else. For several years there after they made me a pro, I didn't get to win a single championship in the few tournaments I competed in.

I had to stay professional, because I needed the money. But when I married George, that problem ended. He was a top bean in the wrestling business. He was one of the wealthy wrestlers, like Jimmy Londos and Ed Lewis, and he'd been

119

making good business investments. George could see that what I really wanted in golf was to compete and win championships. So he set out to see if we could get my amateur standing back.

We talked about it to people such as our friend Pardee Erdman, who'd played with us the day we first met in the 1938 Los Angeles Open. He was a West Coast officer of the USGA. Darsie L. Darsie, golf writer for the Los Angeles Herald, was another man who advised us. And there were a couple more who helped us with information and references.

We found out that I'd have to apply for reinstatement before I'd been a professional five years. This meant I had to do it before May of 1940. Then I'd have to go through a three-year grace period, laying out of all professional things. That wouldn't be easy, but I was willing to go through with it. I was ready to do whatever it took to get me eligible for all those golf tournaments.

I needed four letters of endorsement from people who were prominent in amateur golf. We were able to get some fine letters. And my application went off to the USGA in January of 1940. I wrote a long letter to Joe Dey, the executive secretary of the USGA. I told him I certainly wasn't enjoying being a professional, and that I'd much rather be competing for the fun of the game than just playing for money. Which was true. The money had always come second with me. The money had been necessary, but what I really loved was the sport itself.

The USGA agreed to restore my amateur standing if I went through the three-year waiting period. I settled down to sweat it out. I dropped all my professional contracts and appearances, and when I entered the occasional open tournaments that I was eligible for, I told them to count me out on any prize money.

The two big ones for me were still the Western Women's Open and the Texas Women's Open. I'd missed them both in 1939, because George and I were out of the country, but I was back in there shooting for those titles in 1940.

The Western Women's Open was held in Milwaukee that year at the Blue Mound Golf and Country Club. I hadn't succeeded in getting past the semifinals in this tournament the three previous times I'd tried it.

I really had myself a time in that 1940 Western. I even caused some excitement in a practice round by shooting a seventy-five, which was women's par at Blue Mound. In the qualifying round I slipped to an eighty-one, but I was still only two strokes away from winning the medal.

On the first day of match play I was paired against an Iowa girl, Phyllis Otto, who was only fifteen years old then, but a real comer. I shot a seventy-eight, the best score of the day, and beat her by six-and-four. I kept on going from there. One day I had a seventy-three to set a new Wisconsin women's record, and then I broke the record in another match with a seventy-two. I beat Mrs. J. A. Ochiltree, Mrs. F. W. Zimmerman and Georgia Tainter to reach the semifinals.

There I met Dorothy Foster of Springfield, Illinois. She'd eliminated me from this same tournament back in 1937. I didn't have a very good day against her in the 1940 tournament, either. We were all even after nine holes. Then I pulled a little ahead. I went two up on her at the fifteenth. On the sixteenth she made a real bid with a birdie, but I holed out a ten-footer to score a birdie myself. Another birdie on the seventeenth gave me the match by three-and-one.

In the finals I was up against Mrs. Russell Mann, the Wisconsin state champion. This was her home course we were playing on. But I wanted this title so bad I could taste it. It was my first chance to win a golf tournament in five years— my last one had been the 1935 Texas state women's championship.

Mrs. Mann kept the pressure on me all the way. It was a thirty-six hole match, and she was one up at the end of the morning round. In the afternoon I caught up to her and slowly pulled away. It was the first nine holes in the afternoon that did it—I shot a thirty-six. I closed out the match on the thirty-second hole to win by five-and-four.

It was October before my other big one of the year came up—the Texas Women's Open at Fort Worth. I went to the finals there against Betty Hicks. I was erratic that day, and she was playing a very steady game. After twenty-five holes it looked as though I was going to blow this one. Betty had me four down. But I made up all those holes by the time we reached the thirty-second. I got a par to win the final hole and take the match by one up.

This gave me a "little slam" of my two major 1940 tournaments. I could hardly wait for my amateur standing to return, so that I could begin going after all the top championships. Meanwhile, with my golf playing cut down so much, I'd already started in on something else during my waiting period. I took up tennis. This was a game I'd never competed in either as an amateur or a pro. I wanted to see whether I couldn't work my way to the top in one more sport.

CHAPTER 10

The shoulder kink that had stopped me when I first started to learn tennis in Dallas a year or two after the 1932 Olympics was all straightened out by the time I took up the game again in California in 1940. Time had taken care of that shoulder. It was completely well again. Now I could make the long reach back on the service, and hit all the other strokes. It was the serving that my shoulder had interfered with the time before.

George arranged for me to get my tennis lessons from the finest teacher—Eleanor Tennant at the Beverly Hills Tennis Club. Teach Tennant, they call her. She's taught so many of the top women players, from Alice Marble to Little Mo Connolly.

When I go into a sport, I don't do it halfway. I went all out on my tennis, just the way I had in the past on basketball and track and golf. I played as many as sixteen and seventeen practice sets in a day. There was hardly a day when I didn't wear holes in my socks, and I ran the soles off one pair of tennis shoes after another.

George thought I was going at it too hard. He was running a custom-tailor shop then in Beverly Hills, just a short walk from the tennis club. He'd come over half a dozen times a day to watch me working out. He'd tell me I should take a little rest, and I'd say, "Rest? I've got another set to play."

Sometimes George got a little angry with me, and with Eleanor Tennant. She'd tell him, "If Babe is going to be a top player, she'll have to practice all the time." And of course I felt exactly the same way about it. That's always been my own theory about any sport.

Eleanor Tennant is a lovely player herself. When we first started I thought she was a great player. I'd watch those strokes of hers, and think "Oh, if I could only play like that!" Then I got to where I could beat her, and I realized that if I didn't get better than that, I wouldn't be able to win anything at all.

I kept improving and improving. I was practicing against some of the outstanding men players from the movie colony, like Paul Lukas and John Garfield and Peter Lorre. I played with some of the leading girls in the game, too. Mary Arnold was one, and Louise Brough was another. Louise was coming up in tennis at that time. We played doubles together. Louise and I talked about entering the national doubles some year as partners.

124

In one practice doubles match we beat Pauline Betz and Margaret Du Pont. Both of them have won the national singles championship several times since, and Louise Brough has too.

Finally Eleanor Tennant said, "Babe's ready now to start getting tournament experience." So in the fall of 1941 my entry went in for the Pacific Southwest championships. That's one of the big ones. It's the last major tournament of the year on the American tennis circuit.

Well, my entry was turned down. It was that old issue of professionalism again. It hadn't occurred to me that the question would come up at all in tennis, since I'd never even played the game. But it seems that once you've been a professional athlete in any sport, the tennis people consider you a pro. And there was no way I ever could qualify as an amateur. In tennis, it's "once a pro, always a pro."

Once I knew that I could never compete in tournaments, that took the fun out of tennis for me. It's not enough for me just to play a game. I have to be able to try for championships. So I quit tennis cold. I still have my rackets, but I haven't touched one from that day to this.

Another sport I took up during those years when I was sweating out my golf amateurism was bowling. I first got interested in it a short time before the tennis stopped. George was thinking about buying a bowling alley. He went around looking over different alleys, and I went with him. We must have looked at dozens of bowling places.

We never did buy an alley, but naturally it wasn't long before I decided to take a whack at this game myself. The first night I tried it, I told George that it was a new game for me.

And it was, as far as ever getting to learn it is concerned. I hadn't had a bowling ball in my hand more than two or three times in my life.

After I rolled a few, George said, "Come on, now. Don't give me that stuff about not knowing how to bowl. You're throwing that ball down there like a professional."

I began to put in a lot of long nights at the bowling alleys with George. He was a little afraid at first that the game might be bad for my golf. He thought bowling might overstrengthen my right hand and cause me to hook my shots. But I was sure it wouldn't give me that kind of trouble, and it didn't.

I got instruction from different people. Jo Pittenger at the Llo-Da-Mar alleys was one of them. I started off throwing a straight powerhouse ball, but I saw that the best players rolled a hook ball and were spot bowlers. So I converted to that style myself.

In bowling I could get the competition I wanted. It didn't matter here whether I was an amateur or professional athlete. I bowled for teams in different leagues there in Los Angeles. I was on the King's Jewelry team in the Southern California Major League. I was their "anchor woman."

One night the five of us set a record with a combined score of 2765 for a block of three games. I had the highest single-game score with 237. Another night I bowled three straight games that were well up in the 200's. My three-game total was over 700. My game average there in the Southern California Major League was over 170.

George and I met a lot of the people in bowling. At one time or another I bowled with just about all the top men stars—Andy Varipappa, Joe Wilman, Hank Marino. And Harold Lloyd, the big Hollywood comedy star of the silent-movie days, was an avid bowler. We got to know him well.

Of course, I was playing some golf right along too. I wasn't going to let myself get rusty at my favorite sport. There was an occasional tournament I could enter. In March of 1941, for instance, they had a women's open at San Francisco. I won that, and I had to get by some good golfers to do it— girls like Marion Hollins and Dorothy Traung. In the finals I edged out Barbara Beach Thompson by three-and-two.

When there was no golf tournament for me to play in— which was most of the time—I made a point of getting in a good three or four practice rounds a week. One day everything was clicking for me and I shot a sixty-four at the Brentwood Country Club. That was the best score that had ever been turned in there by either a man or a woman.

Another time I was paired with Sam Snead in a pro-lady tournament at Inglewood. It was an alternate-shot tournament. That means that on one hole he'd hit the drive, then I'd play the second shot, and he'd hit the third. You'd keep taking turns like that until the ball was in the cup. Then on the next hole I'd have to make the tee shot, and Sam the second, and so forth.

In some of those pro-lady tournaments you'd play a modified form of alternate shots. You'd have a selective drive. Both of you would hit tee shots, and you could choose the one you wanted, and then start your alternating.

But in this tournament at Inglewood that I'm talking about, it was straight alternate shots all the way. And Sam and I got around the course in sixty-eight strokes. I believe that's still the record score for pro-lady alternate shots.

It was a thrill for me to set that record with Sam Snead. It was a thrill just to play alongside him, because he is the most wonderful-looking golfer that I have ever seen. I was really awed watching that swing of his—so intricate and yet so smooth. He's got the most beautiful pivot and the most natural golf swing in the game.

His swing is just perfect. If Sam Snead had the thinking head that Ben Hogan has, then nobody would ever touch him. But little things seem to affect Sam. I've seen him falter in spots where there was no real reason for it—just some idea that got into his head.

Take his putting. A lot has been written about Sam Snead being shaky on putts. Actually Sam is a fine putter. What a lot of the golf fans and newspaper men don't take into account is that Sam hits that ball to the pin so often, he's putting for birdies all the time. And you just can't make all the birdies.

But Sam has this reputation for blowing putts, and sometimes when he's in a position where he only needs to sink a little two-footer, it seems like he gets to worrying about it. And then he does blow the putt.

He's missed winning the National Open so many times that I'm afraid he never will do it. It's in his mind that the Open is his jinx tournament. I hope he does come through one of these years. I know that people in golf will be tickled to death if Sam Snead finally wins a National Open. He's won everything else.

I gave up all paid appearances during my waiting period, but I played some benefit exhibitions, especially for war charities after the United States got into World War II. George kept trying to enlist. He wanted to teach the boys unarmed defense—those wrestling holds of his, you know. If he got in, I planned to take a commission in the Wacs. But one branch of the military services after another turned George down because of varicose veins.

George had switched over to the promotional end of wrestling by this time. He was staging matches at the Olympic Auditorium in Los Angeles. I'd kept after him to quit the ring. I never could stand to watch George wrestle. It looked so rough, and the crowds would get so wild.

I appeared in a number of wartime exhibition golf matches with Bing Crosby and Bob Hope. Bing was the best player of all the Hollywood actors, but Bob was coming right along. I wouldn't know which is the best today. It was a scream, playing with those two. Bob is funnier than Bing, because Bing is a little more conservative and a little more concerned with his golf. But there wasn't a minute Bob Hope was on the golf course that he wasn't clowning. The people really enjoyed it.

I made a good stooge for Bob every now and then myself. Bob would say, "There's only one thing wrong about Babe and myself. I hit the ball like a girl and she hits it like a man."

I remember one match where I teamed up with Patty Berg against Bing and Bob at the San Gabriel Country Club. Patty and I beat them, although nobody out there was too much concerned about the score.

I smacked one about 280 yards off the first tee. Bob Hope dropped to the ground and began beating on it with his hands, pretending to cry and wail.

Bing put on an act of consoling Bob, then Bing took his drive. It was a good bit shorter than mine. So Bob started consoling Bing.

On one of the holes, my second shot bounced into a bunch of people standing near the green. The ball hit a woman's hand. They tell me it knocked a diamond out of the ring on her finger. Anyway, it bounced right back on the green as nice as anything, and rolled up to the pin to give me an easy birdie three.

Bob Hope turned to the gallery. "Now do you see what we're up against?" he said.

At the halfway point the announcer began reciting, "Scores for the first nine holes. Miss Berg, thirty-seven. Mrs. Zaharias, thirty-five. Mr. Crosby, thirty-eight. Mr. Hope—."

Before he could get any farther Bob burst out singing, "I dream of Jeanie with the light brown hair."

Bob Hope made a big production out of lining up one eight-inch putt and sinking it. On another hole he had an eight-foot putt. He missed it, took a second putt, and didn't quite make it that time either.

"This is still the same man putting," he said before he took his third try.

The match closed with the announcer reading off the final scores. And again, before he could get Bob Hope's score out, Bob was back in there singing, "I dream of Jeanie with the light brown hair."

I played benefits for the different armed-service charities with other Hollywood celebrities who were pretty good golfers, like Mickey Rooney and Johnny Weismuller. I also appeared with some of the biggest men's golf stars. Byron Nelson was one. He was on the top of the heap during most of those war years. And Ben Hogan was on his way to the top, although he was off in the Navy part of the time. I think I played with Ben about three times on the West Coast, and once in Chicago.

My idea still was that the more I got to play with the

men, the better it would be for my golf game. My husband George thought so too. Occasionally George and I would enter something like a pro-amateur-lady tournament together. I remember one we were in that was held at the Recreation Park course in Long Beach.

Those tournaments were a little complicated. Three of you played together—a man pro, a woman, and a man amateur. It was best-ball scoring. And the same person could enter in more than one threesome.

In that Long Beach tournament, I was entered in two different combinations. In both of them, Bill Nary was the pro and I was the lady. In one of them George was the amateur. In the other the amateur was a fellow named Oscar Olson.

It was a thirty-six-hole tournament. Well, I wound up both in first place and in second place. Our "team" with Oscar Olson finished first with a best-ball score of 120. The one with George tied for second with 122.

All the time I was doing this sports stuff out there on the West Coast, I was also enjoying being Mrs. George Zaharias. That's what I've been ever since we were married, whether I was keeping house or playing in a golf tournament. I've always competed as Mrs. Zaharias, not Babe Didrikson. George and I are a team.

George has done so much to boost my career along. He's been a good judge of what things would help to build my reputation, and what things wouldn't. I lean a lot on his advice. And I listen to him about my golf playing, too. George has studied golf a lot, and not so much to improve his own game as to be able to help me with my game. And he does know my game today probably better than anyone.

I had a great time fixing up our first real home in West Los Angeles when we settled down there after our trip to Australia. It was a nice little duplex with a yard. I loved the cooking and the housekeeping and the sewing. We bought a sewing machine—I'd always wanted one of my own. I made my own drapes and bedspreads and things. And I had a great time fixing up the yard. I cut the grass myself, and I planted flowers. I put in rose bushes. Every house we've lived in, I've gone in for those rose bushes.

On January 21, 1943, my amateur standing came back in golf. I don't think I've ever been happier in my life. Of course, most of the big tournaments had been suspended for the duration of the war. But from now on, I was eligible to enter all the tournaments there were.

My first appearance as an amateur was in a special thirty-six-hole charity match they arranged the next month between me and the California state women's champion, Clara Callender. It was held at the Desert Golf Club in Palm Springs. I couldn't have asked for a better start. Clara scored a pair of seventy-twos, which is real fine shooting. But I had a seventy in the morning round and a sixty-seven in the afternoon, which broke the course record. I took the match by a margin of four-and-two.

A week or so later both of us entered the midwinter women's golf championship at the Los Angeles Country Club, and we wound up opposing each other again for the title. Neither of us had any trouble on our way to the finals. I shot a seventy-nine in the qualifying round, and then improved on that score every day. I hit women's par of seventy-seven in winning my first match. I had a seventy-four the next day, and then a seventy-three in the semifinals the day after that.

This tournament was at the Los Angeles Country Club's north course, which is longer and harder than the course where Clara Callender and I had played our first match. Clara and I didn't get the kind of scores this time that we'd had at Palm Springs, but we didn't do too bad either.

I had a seventy-six for the first eighteen holes. That was three strokes better than her, although I was only one up at the end of the round. The thing I remember best is that I shot a double-eagle on the tenth hole, where women's par was five. The hole was 405 yards, and it ran uphill. I had a tee shot of more than 250 yards. I used a six-iron on my second, and darned if that ball didn't drop on the green and trickle right into the cup.

Clara Callender had gone one hole ahead of me before that. She never held the lead again, although she hung in there. During the afternoon round she took only one hole, the next-to-last one, but most of the time she was getting halves. My final margin was four-and-three.

Then there were some other women's tournaments they put on in Southern California, and I was able to win just about all of them. In between I kept drilling and drilling on my game, to be ready whenever the regular golf circuit was able to resume again.

At this time I was doing a lot of my practicing as a guest out at the Hillcrest Country Club, which happens to have a Jewish membership. Now that sort of thing means absolutely nothing to me. I've never been able to understand why some people attach importance to what religion the other fellow belongs to. In the sports world you learn right off, if you didn't already know it, that once the competition starts, your creed can't help you or hurt you. It's what you are and what you do that counts.

The only reason I mention it at all is that I want to tell a little story. Out there at Hillcrest one day, the president of the club came up to me. He was a real nice fellow. I got to know him well. Anyhow, he was shaking his head and pretending to look severe.

"I don't know what we're going to do about you," he said. "You're out here almost every day. Guess we'll have to declare you an honorary member of our faith and have you join the club."

At Hillcrest I played golf a couple of times with Joe Louis, who was in his prime then as heavyweight boxing champion of the world. He was a fine gentleman and a good sport—the kind of fellow you enjoy playing golf with. He was a pretty fair golfer, too. He was capable of shooting in the middle seventies, and maybe better than that sometimes, if he had his game going good.

A number of people who are famous for other things might have been championship golfers if they'd made golf their business. I played with General Omar Bradley once after the war at the Indian Creek course in Miami Beach. We were both shooting from the back tees and everything, and he turned in a seventy-five.

During the war years, a civilian couldn't do much traveling around. In 1944 I did get out to the Western Women's Open, which was about the most important of the tournaments that kept going through the war. I'd won it as a pro in 1940, and now I won it as an amateur. I took the trophy with

134

a seven-and-five victory over Dorothy Germain—she's Mrs. Mark Porter now.

In June of 1945 I came back to defend my Western Women's Open title at Indianapolis. I was hitting the ball good. I'd just finished winning a match when I got a phone call from George in Denver. At this time he was switching his wrestling promotions over from Los Angeles to Denver. We were in the process of moving to Denver.

George had bad news. He told me that my sister Esther Nancy had just called from California to say that my mother had been rushed to the hospital. She already was suffering from diabetes, and now she'd had a sudden heart attack. She was in real bad shape. They were afraid she might not pull through.

CHAPTER 11

It just broke me up when I got the word in Indianapolis during the 1945 Western Women's Open that my mother was critically ill in the hospital. I'd always been so close to Momma. After that bad news, I didn't feel like playing golf any more. I told George on the phone that I'd come right back, but he said, "Your Momma wants you to finish the tournament."

I phoned my sister Nancy, who was with her, and she told me the same thing. I'd have gone back anyway, but with the wartime travel priorities still on, I couldn't get a seat on any plane or train out of Indianapolis. So I went through with my quarterfinal match the next day. I sure didn't have my heart in it, but somehow I played well enough to win.

That night Nancy called and told me that Momma had died. I said, "I've got to get back." Nancy said, "You go ahead and win that tournament. That's the way Momma would want it."

Again I tried to get transportation out of there, and again I failed. By now there must have been a half a dozen big shots there in Indianapolis who were trying to get me on a plane for the West Coast, and they couldn't do it. Even with my personal emergency, I didn't rate a high enough priority.

So I played in the semifinals against Mrs. Marge Becker. A lot of times I'd have to step away and wipe my eyes before I could putt. What kept me going was that I felt I was playing for Momma now. It was an eighteen-hole match, and for a while it seesawed back and forth. After twelve holes we were all even. Then I took the next four holes to come out ahead by four-and-two.

When I went out for the finals the next day against Dorothy Germain, the same girl I'd beaten in the deciding match of this tournament the year before, I was really inspired. I set a new women's record for the course—it was the Highland Park Golf and Country Club—with a seventy-two in the morning round. That put me five up. Dorothy staged a good rally in the afternoon and cut into my lead some. I won the match, though, four-and-two.

It wasn't until five o'clock the next morning that I finally was notified that they had a seat on a plane for me. I went as far as Kansas City, and then I was "bumped" off the plane by someone with a higher priority. I sat around the airport for hours, waiting for some plane space to open up. I'd doze off for a while, and then come to with a start. I'd rush up to the ticket counter, thinking they'd forgotten I was there. But they hadn't forgotten. They just didn't have anything for me.

At last I did get on a plane. This time I made it to Albuquerque, New Mexico, before I was bumped again. There was another long layover there. I even tried chartering a plane, but it wasn't possible—they didn't have the gasoline for that. George was working on the phone from Denver, trying to help me through contacts of his. He wasn't having any luck either.

Then a seat opened up on a flight that took me to Phoenix, Arizona. After one last wait, I went on through to Los Angeles. They'd held off the funeral as long as they possibly could, and I just did arrive in time. It happened to be my birthday, June twenty-sixth. The rest of the family was already there. They met me at the airport in Los Angeles, and took me to the chapel where Momma was laid out.

Poppa had died of a heart attack about two years before. I remember that the rest of us were crying and everything, but I noticed that Momma wasn't. I couldn't understand it, as much as she and Poppa had meant to each other for so many years. I said, "Momma, why aren't you crying?" She said, "Babe, if I cried, then you children would start fussing over me. I want you to cry for Poppa."

Well, I never could cry too easy when I was a kid, but when I saw Momma there that day in 1945, I really broke down. The others just left me alone in the chapel to cry it out.

That fall I won my second Texas Women's Open title, beating Mrs. Albert Becker, seven-and-six, and at the end of 1945 a nice thing happened. I was picked as the "Woman Athlete of the Year" in the annual Associated Press poll. I'd

138

won it back in my Olympic year of 1932, but this was the first time I'd been picked since then. During all those years in between, what with my troubles over professionalism and everything, I hadn't been able to compete enough to establish whether I was the No. 1 woman athlete.

I've taken that AP award a total of six times by now, and in 1950, when they had a special fifty-year poll, I was selected the Woman Athlete of the Half Century. Every time it's been a thrill, but I got a special charge out of that 1945 award, because it had been so many years since I'd had this recognition.

The citation covered a couple of my 1945 doings that I haven't mentioned. It said: "Although Mrs. Zaharias first won fame as a track star and later competed in most sports as an amateur and professional, she now concentrates on golf. It was in that field that she was outstanding during the '45 campaign.

"In addition to defeating Betty Jameson in a seventy-two-hole challenge match at Los Angeles and San Antonio, Mrs. Zaharias became the first woman to capture three Western Open golf titles. Although she was upset by Phyllis Otto in the Western Amateur, she bounced back to cop the Texas Open."

In 1946 all the golf tournaments started up again. There was a whole string of them during the summer, ending with the National Women's Amateur the last week in September. That was the biggest one. The National Women's Open was just getting started. It hadn't become the top tournament that it is today, now that the United States Golf Association sponsors it as well as the men's National Open.

I'd never played in the National Women's Amateur, first

because of being declared a pro and later because the tournament was suspended during the war. Here my goal for years and years had been the national championship, and I'd never even had a chance to try for it.

I started a little slow there in 1946. In June I got edged out of the Western Women's Amateur in the semifinals by a girl named Mary McMillin. That was the last losing I was going to do for a long time.

My next tournament was the Trans-Mississippi, which was held in Denver that year. I went all the way this time, beating Polly Riley in the finals, six-and-five. Soon after I went over to Colorado Springs and won the Broadmoor Invitation Match Play tournament. My final opponent was Dorothy Kielty, and the score was six-and-four.

The last appearance I made before the 1946 National Women's Amateur was in George S. May's "All-American Championship" at the Tam o' Shanter Country Club in Niles, Illinois. Later on George added a "World Championship" for both men and women to his "All-American" tournaments. That Tam o' Shanter competition was a happy hunting ground for me for many years, starting back there in 1946, when I won the women's branch of the All-American. It's a medal-play tournament. I had a four-round total of 310 strokes. I've improved on that score considerably in later tournaments there.

So I came into my first National Women's Amateur with a winning streak of three straight tournaments. The scene of the National that year was the Southern Hills Country Club in Tulsa, Oklahoma. It was a long course—a good tee-shot course. I always like that kind.

I was pointing for this tournament, all right. You could

say I'd been pointing for it more than thirteen years, from the time I first took up golf seriously. It would be a terrible thing to go through an entire golf career without ever winning the National. And that's happened to some fine players, such as Maureen Orcutt. It's so easy for upsets to happen in a match-play tournament like that. Almost always there are unknowns who catch fire and put out some of the favorites.

Although I didn't know it, 1946 was going to be my one and only chance to take the National Women's Amateur championship. Well, my performance that week was everything I could have hoped for. There was a thirty-six-hole qualifying round, in which I placed third, and my game just built up from there. I didn't have a single narrow squeak in working my way to the finals, although I had to get past some tough competitors, including Peggy Kirk and Maureen Orcutt and Helen Sigel.

On the last day I was opposed by the girl I'd had those two close matches with in California right after my amateur standing came back in 1943. She was Clara Callender then; now she was Mrs. Sherman.

This time it wasn't close. I was hot. She wasn't. We were even through the first six holes. After that I was ahead all the way. At lunch time I was five up. It only took nine more holes in the afternoon to finish things. I won the eighth with an eagle—my 130-yard second shot went in the cup for a two. I took the ninth with a par to end the match. My winning margin of eleven-and-nine was the second biggest in the history of the tournament.

What gave me the most satisfaction, next to winning my first national championship, was that I hadn't played any bad golf at all that week. I don't really enjoy a tournament, even

141

if I win, unless I play well. Sometimes you hit a ball, and you don't hit it the way you wanted to, but it goes on the green anyhow. You were lucky. I don't like it that way. I'm never really satisfied unless I can feel that I'm hitting the ball just right.

After the National, I won the Texas Women's Open in October, beating Betty Hicks in the final, five-and-three. Then I went home to stay a while. We were all settled in Denver now. George had his wrestling matches going good there, and he was staging some boxing shows too. When we first moved to Denver we lived in a hotel, but now we'd bought a home—the first full-fledged house we'd ever owned. I put in the prettiest rose garden I've had. This was a beautiful old English house. I'd said when we got it, "This is it. I'll never want to move out of this house."

When I came back there at the end of the tournament season in October, I was ready to take a long layoff from golf competition and just enjoy my home for a while. But George had other ideas. He said, "Honey, you've got something going here. You've won five straight tournaments. You want to build that streak up into a record they'll never forget. There are some women's tournaments in Florida at the start of the winter. I think you should go down there."

George said he'd come with me to Florida, and then at the last minute he couldn't, what with his promotions in Denver. So he just went with me as far as Pueblo. We spent the night there with his mother and dad. The next day he went to Denver, and I took off in the car toward Florida.

I must have gone about 150 miles, and then I turned around and drove straight back home to Denver. George was in the house. He said, "What are you doing here?"

I said, "The farther I got down the road, the more lonesome I got. I'm not going to go."

But I finally did hit the Florida tournaments near the end of January, and later on George was able to join me for some of the tour. He always has traveled the circuit with me as much as he possibly could. Believe me, it helps to have him right there pulling for me, and it's nice to be able to talk with him after the day's play is over.

George is a combination coach and trainer when he's with me at a golf tournament. He knows better than to over-advise you. He doesn't keep harping on little details. If he notices some tiny flaw, but it's not really hurting my play, then he won't even mention it while the tournament is on. And he can give the best rubdowns. He knows just how to work the soreness out of an athlete's muscles.

On that 1947 Florida trip I was playing a tournament a week. I started with the Tampa Women's Open. It was four rounds of medal play, and at the end of three rounds I was only one stroke ahead of Louise Suggs. Then on the fourth day I shot two under women's par to finish on top by five strokes.

The next one was a match-play tournament at the Miami Country Club—the Helen Lee Doherty Women's Amateur. I was two strokes under men's par for the entire week. In the qualifying round I had a sixty-eight, which was eight below women's par, four below men's par and only one stroke above the men's record for the course. Jean Hopkins and Mary Agnes Wall gave me close matches along the way, but I won the final against Margaret Gunther by twelve-and-ten.

The week after that I went to Orlando and won the Florida Mixed Two-Ball Championship in partnership with

Gerald Walker, the big-league ballplayer. Gee Walker, they call him. We beat Polly Riley and Joe Ezar in the finals. The match ended on the thirty-first hole.

Now my winning streak was up to eight straight tournaments. I believe that was already a record in major golf competition. I still wasn't taking it all as seriously as George was, though. Talking to him in Denver by telephone after that Orlando tournament, I told him, "I'm tired of traveling around down here by myself. I'm ready to come home."

"No, honey," he said. "Don't do that. You're in a hot streak. Stay with it." And he talked me into sticking it out by myself for another week or two. He said that he'd be able to break away from Denver by then and join me in Florida. And he did get down a couple of weeks later.

So I moved on to the Palm Beach Women's Amateur, and just barely kept my string unbroken in the finals against Jean Hopkins. She had me two down with three holes to play. Then I managed to take every one of those last three holes and finish one up on her.

There was quite a rhubarb over the wind-up to the next tournament, the Women's International Four-Ball at Hollywood, Florida. It was Peggy Kirk and I against Louise Suggs and Jean Hopkins, and after thirty-five holes we were all square. It was almost dark. There was some discussion about whether we should try to play any more, but finally they had us drive off the last tee.

We never did play out the hole. Everybody drove, but only a couple of us took our second shots. There was a question of whether someone in the gallery had picked up one of those second shots, or thrown it on the green, or what not. Part of

144

the gallery was hollering that the match should be stopped, and others were hollering for us to play it out. Finally they did call off the match.

The next day we had an eighteen-hole playoff, and with Peggy Kirk shooting some fine golf for our side, we won by four-and-two.

That was victory No. 10. I won't bother going into details on every tournament in my streak. No. 11 was the South Atlantic Women's Championship at Ormond Beach—I beat Peggy Kirk, five-and-four. No. 12 was the Florida East Coast Women's Championship at St. Augustine, where I scored over Mary Agnes Wall in the finals, two-and-one.

There was a short layoff before No. 13—the Women's Titleholders Tournament at Augusta, Georgia. That's the little sister to the Masters Tournament. It was the first time I'd played in it. After two rounds of medal play Dorothy Kirby was ten strokes ahead, but at the end, I was on top by five strokes with 304. I pulled the tournament out with a seventy-one the third day and a seventy-four the last day.

The Titleholders is a wonderful tournament. It's golf as golf should be played. The ball is never touched. On the winter tour a lot of courses aren't in the best of shape, and you're allowed to move the ball out of bad spots on the fairway, and things like that. But I know the galleries don't always understand this. It makes a better impression when you just play the ball as it lies. That's the way the Titleholders is run, in good weather or bad.

For No. 14 I went up to Pinehurst, North Carolina, in the middle of April for the North and South Women's Amateur. I got to the finals against Louise Suggs, who is a very fine golfer and doesn't make many mistakes. She's extra tough on a short course like Pinehurst. I believe she was shooting the finest golf of her career around that period.

Going into the last hole, I was one up on her. I pushed my tee shot over to the right of the green in front of a tree. The ball was so close to the tree that if I tried to chop it out, I was going to hit the tree trunk on my backswing, and probably mess up my shot. So I tried a pool type of shot. I turned around and hit the ball against the tree. I was going to bounce it back as far as I could. Maybe I'd get lucky and bounce it on the green.

But I didn't get lucky. The ball hit a wrong angle on the tree and kicked over to the right. I went over there kind of upset and mad at myself, and reached down too fast to pick some pine straws out of the way. I moved my ball, which cost me another stroke. I wound up with a five, while Louise came out of a bunker to get down in four and square the match.

Well, that almost killed me, and George, who was there watching, was just going crazy. He told me after, "I thought for sure you were going to lose one and break that string." But I knocked in a good putt on the first extra hole for a half, and then on the second extra hole I knocked in a real good putt for a birdie to win.

After that tournament I was really ready to go home and see my flowers and work around the house and garden. It was a month before I played again—in the Celebrities Tournament in Washington, where I won the women's division for No. 15.

In the meantime, George has been doing some more of his thinking about my future. "Honey," he says, "you want to go over to Scotland and play in the British Women's

146

Amateur in June. You need something like that to top off your streak, the way Bobby Jones went over and played those British tournaments the year he made his grand slam."

I said, "I won't go unless you go with me."

He said, "Sure, honey, I'll go with you. I'll make it if I possibly can."

I said, "I know you. You're giving me some more of that old con. You won't go. You'll never be able to get away for that long."

George kept coming back to the subject as the days went on. At one point we ran into Tommy Armour, one of the real great golfers, and George got Tommy to talk to me about it.

Tommy Armour is another of the men who helped me to build my golf game. When I was first under contract with Goldsmith, I was hitting the ball long but my accuracy wasn't too good. They arranged for me to take a course of lessons from Tommy Armour. I think it was in 1937. I went to the Medinah Country Club in Illinois, where he was the pro.

The Medinah Open was on. I was all dressed up, wearing my girdle and everything. I had on kind of a tight skirt and blouse. There were little wooden buttons all down the front of the blouse. I was in stockings and high-heeled shoes.

I was anxious to meet Tommy Armour. The great names of golf fascinated me, and of course I aspired to be one of them myself. I went down to where he was and introduced myself. He was at the practice tee giving a lesson—sitting down, as he usually does.

He said, "Mildred, let me see you hit a ball." He never would call me Babe. He's always called me Mildred.

I said I didn't think I could swing a club, dressed up the

147

way I was, but he told me to go ahead and try one. Well, there was a cyclone fence about 200 yards from the practice tee. I drew back and hit the ball clear over it. I busted most of the buttons on my blouse while I was doing it.

He said, "Well, it's true. They said you could hit a ball pretty far. There aren't many people who carry the ball over that fence."

He told me to hit a few more, so I took off my high-heeled shoes and started banging away in my stocking feet. Tommy Armour gave up all his other lessons for a while and just worked with me every day. I think it was two-and-a-half or three months that I worked with him there. He helped me a lot, especially on my iron play. He was noted for being a great iron player. And I've always thought a lot of Tommy Armour.

So here it is 1947, and George and I are talking to Tommy. George says to him, "Do you think Babe should go to Scotland for the British Women's Amateur this year?"

Tommy is an old Scotsman himself. He turns to me. "Mildred," he says, "you go!"

That was one of the things that finally decided me. George wasn't able to make the trip with me, but I went anyhow. I was to find that nothing I'd done in golf in the past was anything like playing this tournament. I've never had such an experience!

CHAPTER 12

There was never any event that was more important for me in sports than the British Women's Amateur golf championship in 1947. I'd already set a record with my string of fifteen straight tournament victories, which had brought me quite a lot of publicity. But that British tournament was to land me on more front pages than the other fifteen put together.

Going over and adding those British championships to their American ones is what has nailed down the reputations of practically all our famous golfers, from Walter Hagen and Bobby Jones and Gene Sarazen to Sam Snead and Ben Hogan. I was trying to do the same thing—to show that I could beat the best on both sides of the Atlantic Ocean. There was one difference about my attempt. A number of our players had won the important British men's tournaments. But no American girl had ever taken the British Women's Amateur from the time it first started in 1893.

My promoter-husband George saw the value of all this, but for a while I couldn't get very excited about it. When we were talking the idea over with Tommy Armour, one of the things I said was, "How do I know whether this tournament will be worth that long trip? Who all's going to be playing in it, anyhow?"

I can't give you Tommy's exact words, but they came to this. "It doesn't matter who's in the tournament. You go. This is the one you must win."

I traveled by myself, since George was tied down by business back home in Denver. I had a smooth crossing over to Southampton, England. After that the trip got a little rough. Things were still tough there in the British Isles that soon after the war.

I came off the boat in Southampton on a real hot, humid day. They said it was the worst heat for that date in sixty-two years, or some such thing. I got on the morning boat train for London, and it was jammed. I was all laden down with things. I had two cameras with me, and my knitting bag, and different pieces of luggage. I was even carrying my fur coat. I had on a suit that turned out to be too warm for the weather that day. And I couldn't get a seat on the boat train. I had to stand all the way from Southampton to London.

At the station in London I rushed out to get a taxicab. I had to get to another depot, the King's Cross Station, and catch a train for Edinburgh in Scotland. There were a lot of people out at the taxi place, too I asked for a cab, and I was told, "Lady, you'll have to wait in queue."

I said, "Queue? What's queue?" And they explained that meant standing in line until my turn came.

About twenty-five cabs later, my turn did come. And three other people jumped into the cab with me. There wasn't even room for me to get all my luggage in. Finally it was arranged that a couple of the people would have to get out and wait for the next cab.

My train for Edinburgh was due to leave a little after one o'clock, as I remember it. I didn't get to King's Cross Station very long ahead of that. On my train trip up from Southampton, I'd just said, "I want a ticket to London." This time I wanted to make sure I got a first-class ticket, so as to have a comfortable seat for the rest of my trip.

I was hurrying in to buy my ticket, and all of a sudden the gates to the station closed on me. I said to a man, "What in the world is this? Why are they closing the gates?"

He said, "The King and Queen are coming." It seems that when that happens, they close off the whole front of the station. The King and Queen arrived in a party of four or five cars, and this long red carpet was rolled out for them to walk into the station. There were bouquets of flowers all around it.

So the King and Queen went into the station, and of course I was thrilled at getting a chance to see them. Then the gates began to open up again, and I started running up that carpet where the King and Queen had gone. I was half-way up, and a man stopped me and said, "Lady, you cannot walk on that carpet. You cannot go that way."

I said, "I'm sorry, but I have to get my ticket. I have to catch that train to Edinburgh."

151

He said, "You must go over to the annex when the King and Queen are here. Nobody is allowed in the station."

I got my ticket at last, and just did make my train. It was loaded with civilians and some men in uniform, the way the boat train had been. And I had to stand on this one too. The first-class compartments were all filled. I asked the conductor, "Doesn't a first-class ticket mean that I get a seat?"

He said, "No, madam. First come first served."

So I stood in the aisle with all my gear. It was hotter than ever. The windows were open—we'd have suffocated otherwise—and soot from the engine was blowing in. There were black specks all over my face and hair. I was dripping all over. My curls had come down. I never did get my hair to stay up right the whole time I was in England and Scotland.

I thought I was going to faint any minute. It was about a nine or ten-hour trip. Whenever anybody left their seat for a few minutes, I'd go sit there until they came back.

After we'd been riding for quite a while they announced the first call for tea. I made a beeline in there and got to sit down. I was going to stay there and order again at the second call, and the third call too. But they told me I couldn't do that. They said you could only sit through one serving. Then you had to leave to give other people a turn.

We finally got to Edinburgh some time after eleven o'clock at night. From then on things couldn't have been nicer. A car was waiting at the station to take me to Gullane, the little town where the tournament was being held.

"Well, thank God!" I said to the driver. "I'm certainly glad to see you." I made myself comfortable in the back seat, and asked him, "How far have we got to go?"

He told me it was a thirty-five or forty minute drive.

I said, "Good." Then I stretched back and went right to sleep. I slept all the way to Gullane.

The car took me to the North Berwick Inn, where I had a reservation. I just loved that little old hotel. They were so hospitable. There was this little guy who was a sort of combination desk clerk and bell boy and everything else. He said he was tickled to meet me, because he'd read a lot about me and was a great fan of mine. And the manager did everything he could to make me comfortable and help me succeed. The food rationing was very tight then, but he'd laid in a supply of special things for me. He'd said, "We want her to have the things she's used to eating."

I went down my first morning and the waiter asked me what I'd like.

I said, "Well, I'd like some bacon or ham and eggs and some fried potatoes and toast and coffee. But I don't suppose I can get that here."

He said, "Mrs. Zaharias, we've got all that. The manager is keeping some chickens out there just for you. And he went to an American boat and got bacon and ham for your whole stay here."

I told him, "That's as nice a thing as I ever heard of." I did feel sort of guilty, though, about taking all this special stuff.

I got over there a few days before the tournament so I could do some practicing. The Gullane golf course was down a quaint little street from the hotel. Everybody rode bicycles around there. They wore those clips on their pants legs. At first I thought I'd get me a bicycle to go to the golf club and

153

back, but then I decided I'd rather walk. I liked to look at the houses with the little stone fences around them, and see the men and the girls and the boys on their bicycles.

I said hello to all of them. They'd say, "Hello, Mrs. Zaharias." I told the newspaper reporters, "I wish you'd ask everybody just to call me Babe." And a number of the people started doing that.

When I walked back to the hotel in the evening, about ten or fifteen women would come out of houses along those four or five blocks and say, "Would you like tea with us?" And several times I said, "Thank you," and went in. Of course, sometimes I couldn't, because I had reporters and photographers waiting for me back at the hotel, and things like that.

One night they had me pose wearing a pair of Stuart Clan kilts. I thought it might be a nice gesture for me to wear those kilts when I played the finals, if I got that far. But I found the kilts were so big and heavy that I just couldn't have played golf in them.

This Gullane was a seaside course. People kept warning me to stay out of "the winds," and I thought they meant the sea breezes. But it turned out that "the winds" were a hedge-like kind of rough. I'm thankful that I never did get in that stuff during the tournament, because it was really mean—all thick and jumbled together.

Gullane was a lot different from our American tournament courses. There were sheep wandering all over the place. The sheep were used to golfers, though. When I came along in a practice round, the sheep would just step aside into a bunker or into the rough.

The sheep were on the greens a lot. The club was giving

me extra courtesies, and when I practiced, they had a fellow in a white coat go along in front of me and clean off the greens where the sheep had been. I believe the average golfer just had to take care of that the best he could.

These courses over there are considered the property of the Scottish people. There was no golf on Sunday, so the people could go out there for picnics and stuff. And you'd see families just taking a stroll on the golf course, or giving their dogs a walk. The dogs would always be on leashes. I never saw a dog in Scotland that wasn't on a leash.

During the war they'd put up tank traps all over the coast for protection in case of invasion. They were big pillars of cement, five feet thick and eight feet long, stuck in the ground so close together that no tank could have got between them. After the war they dug holes and dropped these pillars down into the ground. Most of them were gone from the golf course by the time I got there, but they still had a few down near the shore, where they might have interfered with the play on some of the holes during the tournament. When I got there they were rushing to get rid of the last of the pillars. They had crews of former Polish soldiers who had escaped to England during the war working on the job. Some of the townspeople had to pitch in near the end and help to get the work done in time.

There were no practice fairways or practice tees at Gullane. Over there, I guess, they just practice by playing around the course. Tournament players in this country like to get out in one spot and play the same kind of shot over and over.

The secretary of the club at Gullane saw me one day trying to practice out of the high grass alongside a fairway, and he asked me, "Why don't you go play on the golf course?" I explained what I was doing, and then they fenced off a practice place for me. They let some of the sheep in there, and the sheep cropped that grass down as neat as any mower.

At that time of year it stayed light in Gullane until about three hours after midnight. They put up blackout curtains for me in my room at the hotel so the light wouldn't keep me awake. And before I went to bed, I'd sometimes get in an extra practice round of golf after dinner.

George was phoning me just about every day from Denver—what a phone bill he ran up that month! And he's always been after me not to wear myself out with too much practicing. One night he called, and I said, "Hi, honey. It's eleven o'clock at night here, and I just got in from playing a round."

He said, "Good Lord! Now take it easy, will you?"

Along the first two fairways there was this street, with a lot of big houses lined up on the other side. When I came down those fairways during my practice rounds, there'd be people in the windows of the houses watching me. I always waved to them, and they'd wave back. One family came over and invited me to dinner. I went there a couple of times, and became good friends with them.

And then there was Mrs. Annie Thurban Brown, a golfer at the club. Her husband had been killed in the war, I believe. She had a little daughter eight or nine years old. She was just wonderful to me. She took me places and showed me everything. She helped me with money exchanges and things like that.

I think it was on my second practice round that I got in the tall grass off the fairway on one hole. It was a kind of wet

156

day, and my hands were a little sticky from the dampness. That grass was real long, and it laid down sort of like an Afghan hound's hair.

I went in there to play my ball out. I said to myself, "Well, I've got to learn how to handle this stuff." I caught the ball all right, but the grass wrapped around my club, and the handle banged against my left thumb and chipped a bone there.

Mrs. Brown got a doctor for me. He treated it, and then every morning he'd put something on it to kill the pain, and bandage it with an elastic wrapping so that I could still play golf. I didn't want anybody to think I was trying to build up an advance alibi for myself, so I just wore a glove over it, and nobody noticed that there was anything the matter with my thumb.

That thumb stayed sore as a boil, but I think it actually may have helped me during the tournament. I didn't slug the ball quite so hard, and I had better control of it. I don't believe I missed a fairway on but one of my drives the entire week.

I found the weather over there could change three and four times a day. It might start out real warm, and then in no time it would be awfully cold. I had packed for summer. I thought if I needed anything more I could buy it over in Scotland. I found I couldn't because I had no coupons. Clothes rationing was still on.

I had a lot of things I'd made especially for my trip to Scotland—gabardine pastels, green and pink and white and blue and red skirts. I'd made some culotte skirts. I didn't bring anything warm, though, except a couple of sweaters. One of them was an orange cashmere with angora in it.

Well, I mentioned to the press that I hadn't been prepared for any cold weather. That got into the papers, and during the next few days gifts of heavy clothing just flooded into the hotel. First people nearby were bringing packages on their bicycles, and then stuff started coming by mail. Pretty soon the lobby of the hotel was stacked high with these packages.

I was really touched by the generosity of all those people. I went through a few of the packages and picked out an old siren suit—one of those things the British air-raid workers used to wear—and a pair of blue corduroy slacks. I wrote thank-you notes for those two items, and I asked the newspaper reporters please to publish my thanks to everybody else. The packages that had return addresses I sent back. On the rest I announced that I hoped the people would come and pick them up, because I was sure they could put the clothing to better use somewhere else.

From then on, if I was afraid of bad weather, I'd take the siren suit and slacks out to the course with me and carry them along in my golf bag. If it got a little cold, I'd put on the siren suit. If it got real cold or rainy, I'd slip the slacks on over it. And I already had my cashmere sweater.

When the tournament started on June ninth—that was a Monday—I didn't know what to expect. There was no qualifying or seeding. They just put all the names in a big hat and drew them out. About the only player I was familiar with was another American girl who had come over for the tournament. That was Helen Sigel, of Philadelphia. She's now Mrs. Helen Sigel Wilson. The only other American in it was a girl from Fall River, Massachusetts, named Ruth Woodward, now Mrs. Kip Finch of New Canaan, Conn.

A total of ninety-nine women were entered, and it was the luck of the draw who you came up against. This was one of those sudden-death tournaments. Every day you had to survive two eighteen-hole matches, one in the morning and one in the afternoon. By Thursday the field would be narrowed down to two women for a thirty-six-hole final.

The caliber of my opponents wasn't the only unknown quantity for me in this "Ladies' Amateur Golf Championship Tournament, under the management of the Ladies' Golf Union"—to quote the official British name for it. I was due for all kinds of surprises.

CHAPTER 13

I got out early the morning of my first match in the British Women's Amateur tournament. I expected to see a crowd already gathering, the way it does for an American tournament. But there was hardly a soul in sight.

I said to the club secretary, "I thought Scotland was golf country. Where are all the people?"

He said, "They'll be here." And sure enough, all these buses began coming in, and by the time I teed off there must have been several thousand people there. They didn't come early because there was nothing for them to do at the course. They couldn't go to the clubhouse, naturally. Not even the golf pros were allowed in the clubhouse. I understand that's changing now at the British clubs. Anyway, there were no facilities for the spectators at Gullane, so the people didn't get there until it was time for the matches they wanted to see.

On the first tee there was a sign saying, "No Practice Swing." Well, I never hit practice balls off the tee when I'm about to play a match. If you don't hit one right, then immediately you start trying to correct your swing—and it's too late for that. The most I'll do is chip and putt a little bit before the start of a match.

But I do like my practice swing. It sort of gets me in the groove. Since it was against the rules in this tournament, I got in the habit of going off to one of the few spots where the grass was cropped down enough and taking my warm-up swings there. Then my match would be called, and when I got up on the first tee, I'd sometimes forget and automatically start to take another practice swing. But I always remembered in time and checked myself.

Anyhow, the starting time came for my first match, which was against a girl named Helen Nimmo. And I spotted these two little old Scotsmen sitting on a bench. They were wearing kilts. I'd gone to Scotland with the idea that all the men wore kilts, but I found that wasn't so around Gullane. These two were the first I'd seen. I asked about them later, and was told that they were golf professionals from the North Highlands, where the men do wear kilts right along.

Those two just fascinated me. They were in my galleries all through the tournament. They'd always be sitting on that bench near the first tee, and after my opponent and I drove off, they'd join the crowd and follow me around the course. They'd walk along with their heads close together, gabbing and gabbing, and those kilts would be bobbing up and down.

So my first match began, and I couldn't get over how quiet the gallery was. They were so orderly in moving around the course—there was none of the wild stampeding you sometimes have with American crowds. And they didn't yell or applaud. The most you'd hear would be somebody saying, "Well played," or "Fine shot."

I was saying to myself, "Gee, you have to knock the ball in the hole off the tee to get a hand around here." Well, I clinched that first match on the twelfth hole. And it wasn't until then that they all applauded.

I told Mrs. Helen Holm, a past British Women's Amateur champion, who was acting as a marshal, "I wish these people would just holler and enjoy themselves the way the crowds do back home." And she explained that the Scottish tradition was for the gallery to be very quiet so as not to disturb the players.

But I was going to loosen up those galleries if I could. In my match that afternoon I began kidding them a little. I said, "Come on, let's have some fun." I told them they could make all the noise they wanted to and it wouldn't bother me. I said the noise would make me play better, because it was what I was used to.

My opponent in the afternoon round was Mrs. Enid Sheppard. She gave me a pretty tough match, but I won it on the sixteenth hole, four-and-two. When a match ends like that in an American tournament, we often go ahead and play out the rest of the course. We play the by-holes to give the crowd a little extra show.

I asked Mrs. Sheppard, and I asked Helen Holm, "Would it be all right to play the by-holes?" Mrs. Holm said at first

I don't know where or just when this shot was taken, but I sure dig the fellow I'm "teaching" When it concerns grace, rhythm and power in hitting a golf ball, Sam Snead is my all-time pin-up boy

I've enjoyed a fine association with Serbin, Inc Between us we've turned out some sensible sports shirts for gals who want comfort with grooming

Wilson Sportpix

Male pros have been tinkering with and reworking their clubs for years, but most girls are satisfied to just swing them Not me.

With the gentleman to whom I owe so much, my life in fact Dr W E.
Tatum of Beaumont, my home, and a benign wizard with cancer This
was taken on April 14, 1953, at the Beaumont Country Club, the day
I just lasted to win my last tournament before checking into the Hotel
Dieu Hospital

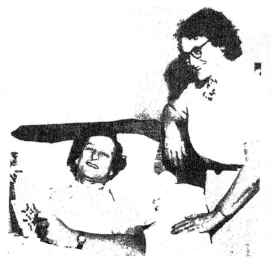

My sister Lillie remained close until they wheeled me into the biggest competitive round of my life Then, when they finally checked me out of the hospital I was invalided at my brother's home in Newton, Texas I was weak and washy but at least the desire to return to golf was burning .and strong! This third picture is triumph of a sort. I'm back in Tampa and helping me to unpack the car is Betty Dodd, a wonderful girl who stuck to me through the roughest going This was on July 3, 1953, and our little home at the Tampa Golf Club sure looked inviting

Fishing at Key Largo with my brother Ole I'm on
the mend here and feeling stronger by the minute
as Betty takes a siesta in the background

Two lost souls I was back on the firing line again 3½ months after my operation. I'd struggled through two mid-80 rounds at the Tam O'Shanter and when I headed for the 6th tee of the 3rd round, I was beginning to doubt everything including my confidence! I guess I started to cry and George, bless him, is trying to comfort me

Fresh start After my little cloudburst I took a fresh tuck in my belt, and the shots started coming off much better. I finished that round with a 78 for 15th place Then a few days later I finished 3rd in the World Championship.

Count your blessings I've made many trips to children's wards since my own recovery Somehow, children accept bitter blows with a near-divine faith

This little beauty is Barbara Ann Scott, who also knows the meaning of relentless work and practice As for Pierre, Barbara's pup—a kibitzer isn't he?

On the pro golf tour, we often bust out and give the customers a little something extra, but I don't think Arthur Godfrey is looking for Betty and me just yet.

Younger than springtime, and that's how I felt after posting a record 69 at Tam O'Shanter in '54 George is a willing stooge here, but believe me, he's a wonderful chef.

With Byron Nelson, a Texas fire horse Byron turned himself out
to competitive pasture some years back but came galloping back
to the fires in '55. His recent victory in the French Open is symbolic.
This was at the Tam O'Shanter a few years back.

Cary Middlecoff may become the heir, in-fact, to Ben Hogan's throne It couldn't happen to a nicer person or a harder-working pro (*Below*) There's a lot of Irish plus Texas-American in Ben Hogan's wonderful smile Ben's the shiningest example of work and more work!

Wide World Photo

Wilson Sporting Goods Co

I like this picture simply because it points up strengths—from the feet on up, in a pretty good golf swing . . . again!

Winning the '54 U S Women's Open was, perhaps, one of the most satisfying victories of my life. As a beacon, it served to blink encouragement to thousands who must battle cancer.

Another thrill was watching our
new home in Tampa take on
shape and character It may not
be "pure" architecture, but for
George and me it's the ultimate
in comfortable living

Roses have always been my favorite flowers and I love growing them

Lon H Wilson

The President is an enthusiastic golfer, Mrs. Eisenhower a gracious First Lady. I may be about to shake Ike's hand at a Washington dinner rally in October '54, but it could be I'm telling him about a 2-foot putt I blew in a recent tournament.

Here, we're teeing off for the Cancer Fund Drive as Mr. President uses the overlapping grip to get the greatest distance out of the initial tee shot.

At the New York Met Golf Writers' dinner in January '55,
Bob Jones congratulates '54 Open champion Ed Furgol
What with Bob's spinal trouble, Ben Hogan's comeback
from that nearly fatal smashup, Furgol's withered left arm,
and my cancer, we all have a vital "something" in common
besides golf And I think it is our burning interest in golf
that has helped us all to live with and to overcome these
"somethings"

In the evenings, the breezes blow in from Tampa Bay and
life can be very restful and beautiful around our home I've
been a wonderfully fortunate girl .. but I don't intend to
ɔast on my good fortunes

that she didn't know whether we should, because that wasn't done in Scotland. But she's spent quite a bit of time in the United States herself, and finally she said to go ahead and do it.

I gave them some of the trick shots I use in exhibitions in this country. There's one where I put a kitchen match on the ground behind my ball on the tee, and when I drive, it sounds like a small cannon being fired, because that match goes off with a loud pop.

I did that off the seventeenth tee, and the ball sailed nearly 300 yards out there and landed in a trap right in front of the green. From the trap I did another of my stunts. I balance one ball on top of the other, which is quite a trick in itself. I swing, and the bottom ball is supposed to go on the green and the top one into my pocket. Well, not only did the one ball jump into my pocket, the other went right into the hole.

By this time the gallery was in an uproar. When I finished out on the eighteenth green by turning around backwards and putting the ball between my legs into the cup, they didn't quiet down for a long time. They kept me out there giving autographs for nearly an hour.

The next day there was a sign on the bulletin board: "Please do not play the by-holes." So I didn't do that any more. But those crowds got bigger and friendlier every day. They sounded almost like the crowds at home by the end of the tournament.

One of the British golf writers, Fred Pignon, headed his story of that first day: OUR GIRLS SHAKEN BY GOLF 'BABE'. He wrote: "Mrs. Zaharias took practically all the spectators and crashed her way over the hills and dales of this testing, undulating course. She tore holes in the rough with tremendous recovery shots, and simply bettered her opponents in both her matches with the most tremendous exhibition of long driving ever seen in women's golf."

There was just one person there that week who seemed to resent my coming over to try and win their championship. That was a woman whose name I've forgotten. She wasn't in the tournament herself, but I believe she was a former player. Well, all of us contestants had cards that admitted us to the clubhouse for tea. I went up there that first afternoon, and this woman invited me to join her.

Of course, I wanted to be friends with everybody, and I sat down with her. And she began telling me, "Did you know that there is a jinx against American women in this tournament? Why, your greatest players have come over here, women like Glenna Collett and Virginia Van Wie, and they've never been able to win."

She went on like that, and she said, "Aren't you worried about the jinx? Do you think you can succeed where all those other fine players have failed?"

I told her, "I didn't come over here to lose," and I broke away as soon as I could without making a scene. That was one woman who didn't speak my language, and I don't mean because of her Scottish accent.

In my two matches the next day I was really on my game. Women's par at Gullane was seventy-six, and men's par was seventy-one. At least, that's the way the experts calculated it. There was no official par for the course.

In the morning against Mrs. Val Reddan, I was even with the men's par through the first nine holes, and only one over it by the fourteenth, where I closed out the match, six-and-four. In the afternoon I shot the first nine in thirty-three—two under men's par. Mrs. Cosmo Falconer had a forty, which was only one over women's par, but she still was five down at the turn. The final score of that match was six-and-five.

Both the other American girls were eliminated that day —Helen Sigel in the morning and Ruth Woodward in the afternoon. That left me as the only one with a chance to bring the United States its first British Women's Amateur title.

Another of the differences I was having to get used to over there was the Scottish caddies. They're elderly men— the one I had looked about eighty years old to me. And they're accustomed to giving the golfers a lot of advice about how to play.

I never take advice from a caddy, other than to ask them about distances and directions if I'm not too familiar with the course. I always plan my own shots and pick my own clubs.

Well, it wasn't long before this old fellow started in telling me what he thought I should do. At first I said to myself, "I'll just ignore him." But then we came to one shot where I wanted to drop the ball on the green with my wedge. And the caddie handed me a three-iron.

I said, "Would you please leave the clubs in the bag and let me pick them out?"

He said, "Madam, the wind is against you. You should take this three-iron and run the ball up there."

I told him, "I don't play two and three-iron pitches on little short shots. I'm used to hitting the ball up in the air." And I finally got to play it my way with the wedge.

Later, there was a story that I went to the caddie master

and asked, "Don't you have any younger caddies here?" And he said, "Yes, Mrs. Zaharias, we'll be glad to get you a younger boy." And he brought out a caddie who was only seventy-five-years old.

Actually I kept my same caddie straight through the tournament. He stopped trying to choose my clubs for me after I asked him not to, and carried my clubs in good style.

On the third day, a Wednesday, I was to play Frances Stephens in the quarterfinals in the morning. If I got by her, I probably would face Jean Donald in the semifinals in the afternoon. That was the match they'd been making a big thing out of in the newspapers. Jean Donald was the Scottish girl who was supposed to have the best chance of beating me and keeping the championship at home.

They were talking it up around the club all week. People would say to me, "You and Jean Donald should have a wonderful match if you come up against each other. She's a fine golfer, and this is her home club. She really knows how to play this course."

Well, they didn't realize it, but that sort of talk just builds me up. The bigger they make a match, the more I get fired up to go out there and show them. It was like the year that the late O. B. Keeler, the well-known Atlanta golf writer, picked Louise Suggs of Atlanta to be the top woman golfer. That got me hustling so much that I had one of my very best years on the tournament circuit.

In the quarterfinals in the morning against Frances Stephens I had my hardest match. I shot men's par for the first nine holes—and she held me even. After thirteen holes I was still even with men's par—and only one up. But I took both the fourteenth and fifteenth holes by a stroke, and then I halved the sixteenth to win out, three-and-two.

In the afternoon against Jean Donald—well, she's a nice girl and a nice golfer, but that wasn't her day. We had a real mob of people following us. The Associated Press account said, "The crowd, attracted by the report that the Scottish champion was out to slay the American champion, grew to almost unmanageable proportions. Estimated by golf writers at between 5000 and 8000, the gallery was the largest of the season—far larger than the crowd which gathered to watch the British men's amateur at Carnoustie two weeks ago. Nearly 100 stewards barely preserved order."

Jean Donald was hitting her drives almost as far as mine for a while, but I beat her with my short game. The match only lasted thirteen holes, and I was one under men's par for as far as we went. I had just one three-putt green, and there were six times when I was able to hole out with a single putt. It ended seven-and-five, which is a runaway score in an eighteen-hole match.

Like any other woman, I'm forever freshening up my lipstick. Coming off the twelfth green I was putting new lipstick on. I was just doing it automatically, not even thinking about it. Well, it happened that I had her six down with six to play at that time. One of the writers said in his story that I was so sure I'd close out the match on the next hole I stopped to put lipstick on to get ready for the photographers.

The photographers swooped down after that next hole, all right. Jean Donald was a real good sport about her defeat. She posed with me dancing the Highland Fling and everything. I had been over to her house for tea and dinner and stuff like that. We had become very good friends. Her father was a doctor.

Another person I saw a lot of that week was the father of Jimmy Thomson, one of our professional stars. Jimmy has always been a great friend of mine in this country, and when he heard I was going to Scotland he said to be sure and look up his dad at the Berwick golf course. So I did. Jimmy's dad was the sportiest looking guy in all of Scotland, wearing these sports jackets and slacks that Jimmy had sent him from the United States.

He walked around with me in every match I played over there. He looked just like Jimmy, and was the same wonderful kind of fellow. He kept talking to me in his Scottish burr, "You're doing fine. You're a beautiful player." He really did a lot to keep me pepped up all through that tournament.

Meanwhile I kept running into that woman I mentioned earlier who tried to get me worried about the "jinx" against American players in the British Women's Amateur. She'd buttonhole me every time she saw me at the club or the hotel and say, "Don't forget about the jinx." Finally some of the other women found out what she was doing. They must have told her she was being unsporting, and to pipe down, because when I saw her in the clubhouse the last day, she just said, "Hello," and nothing more.

I'll have to admit I was thinking about that jinx a little bit the night before the final round. After all, I could get unlucky and have a bad day like anybody else. The girl I was going to play, Jacqueline Gordon, had been the big surprise of the tournament. She wasn't supposed to be one of the top British women players. She wasn't on their Curtis Cup team or anything. But she'd been beating everybody all week long.

I had my dinner down in the hotel dining room, and then went up to my room. They were still knocking themselves out to please me at that little inn. They were running low on bacon, and the chickens weren't laying quite so many eggs, but they still had plenty of the ham. And the maids had been instructed to take my golf clothes and socks and things and launder them whenever I asked. I can't tell you how grateful I felt to those people.

They had put a heater in my room for when it turned cold, and I needed it the night before the finals. I pulled down the blackout shades to keep out that late-evening light. But I couldn't sleep. Finally I got out of bed and put up the shade and sat by the window.

I ordered up some tea. It was brought by the little fellow who doubled as a desk clerk and bellboy and everything. I told him I was kind of upset, and that it was partly because of the unpleasant way that woman had been needling me about the jinx.

He said, "Mrs. Zaharias, don't take any notice of her. Everybody here wants you to win."

Eventually I did go to sleep. When I woke up it was a beautiful morning. Some of the other days the weather had been pretty mean. People thought it must be tough on me having to play under those conditions. Actually I was ready for it. Before leaving the United States, I'd gone out and practiced like mad every time there was bad weather, just to help prepare myself for this tournament on a Scottish seaside course.

The last morning, though, the weather was so lovely that

I dressed in some of my warm-weather clothes. I put on a light skirt with a light sweater, and white golf shoes and white visor. I had a white golf glove with green backing to cover up that injured thumb on my left hand. Oh, I was a doll that morning, I'm telling you!

It was so nice and warm I didn't even bother to take along my siren suit and slacks, which I found out was a mistake. And I was having a little trouble with my golf shoes. I'd brought along a new pair of brown all-weather shoes that I'd had made especially for this trip, but they'd begun to split from getting wet so often out on the course, and then standing by the heater to dry. So I had to switch to an old pair of golf shoes for the final.

I got out there for my match with Jacqueline Gordon, and this time there already was a crowd waiting for us to start. I could still pick out those two little Scotsmen in kilts, though. I got up on the first tee and looked around, and I saw the British flag flying at the top of the flag pole. I stood at attention and saluted it. The crowd applauded.

Then I looked for an American flag, and someone pointed to the roof of the clubhouse. They had this big American flag stretched out there. I turned around and got right down on the ground and salaamed three times. Everybody roared.

So we started to play. Going down the first and second fairways, I waved as usual to everybody in those houses across the street. Only now it was mostly the servants and the children that I was waving to. The other people were at the tournament themselves.

We hadn't been out there long before the weather turned chilly and windy. Pretty soon I was wishing for my cold-weather stuff. All I had along with me in my golf bag was a

170

blue sweater. I didn't burn up the course during that morning round the way I had in practically all my other matches. And Jacqueline Gordon was playing real good. She wasn't a long hitter, but she was consistent. At the twelfth hole she went two up. I squared it at the fifteenth, and we were still all even at lunch time.

When I came off the course for the lunch break, fifty Scotsmen must have told me, "Babe, go git your slocks on. Go git your slocks on." I was going to do that, and I was also going to do something else.

CHAPTER 14

I didn't waste any time getting back to the hotel after my morning round against Jacqueline Gordon in the finals of the British Women's Amateur. Along with getting some warmer clothes, I wanted to try and have my best golf shoes fixed to wear that afternoon. These were the shoes that had cracked because of the dampness.

At the inn they served me a nice lunch in my room. Then I stretched out for a short rest. After a few minutes I got up and dressed. I put on my siren suit and slacks, which I'd failed to take with me during the morning. The newspapers said the next day that I switched to my "lucky slacks." But I didn't do it for luck. I was just cold!

I headed for the shoemaker shop. I'd been told where it was, and also that it was a lady shoemaker. I got there, and she had a sign in her window like others I'd been seeing in shops along the way: "Sorry. Closed. Gone To See The Babe."

When I got to the clubhouse, somebody asked if I'd had my shoes taken care of, and I said, "No, she was closed." Well, somehow the word circulated through the crowd to that lady shoemaker. It wasn't but a few minutes later that she came up to me and said, "Did you have some shoes you wanted fixed?"

I said, "Yes, ma'am, I sure do." And she took my shoes back to her shop and repaired them, and brought them back to me before we teed off. It was such a nice thing for her to do.

I was really feeling good by the time Jacqueline Gordon and I started in again. I said to myself, "I just know I'm going to play a lot better now." I broke our tie on the very first hole in the afternoon. I got a par four and she had a five.

On the second hole, a par five, I had a long drive and then a long second shot that put me on the green. I holed out an eighteen-footer for an eagle three, which of course gave me the hole. When I won the third hole too, with a par five to her six, I knew for sure I was in charge.

Jacqueline Gordon hung in there, but things kept going my way. About the best she could do was to halve some of the holes. Those two kilted Scotsmen were still in my gallery, and gabbing away more excitedly than ever.

On one hole I hit a tremendous tee shot. I really creamed it. Oh, that drive felt good! It left me just a wedge shot to the green. Walking down the fairway, I was close enough to that pair in kilts to hear one of them saying to the other, "I've watched Walter Hagen and Bobby Jones and Gene Sarazen and all those Americans who've played over here, and none of them could hit the ball better than this girl can."

Now that kind of talk is nice to hear. At this point I felt I just had to say something to them. I fell in step behind them and put my arms across their shoulders.

"How would you boys like to see me knock this little wedge shot right in the cup?" I said.

They said—I can't really do that Scotch burr—"Ah! That would be fine!" So I hit the ball, and it banked just a little bit, and stopped right on the edge of the cup. It almost did go in. And you should have seen the expressions on the faces of those two Scotsmen. Their mouths were hanging wide open. Even the kilts had stopped bobbing for a minute. You could see they were thinking, "She can do whatever she wants to with the ball!"

I was five up going into the back nine. Jacqueline Gordon took the next one—it was the only hole I lost that afternoon. I won the hole after that. Then we played three straight halves, which ended the match, since I was five up and there were only four holes left.

The crowd gave me a wonderful ovation when it was over. It seemed like they stood for fifteen minutes and applauded. Then there was more picture-taking and dancing the Highland Fling and signing autographs and everything.

During the autographing I took the glove off my left hand. That was the first time I'd done it. Nobody had seen the bandage on my left thumb until now. It caused something of a sensation. Then the photographers had me go over to the area in front of the clubhouse for pictures, and I hurdled the brown brick wall that ran around it. There was another uproar over that.

Finally there was the presentation of the championship trophy. I sang a little Highland song I'd learned from some of the Scottish golf pros in the United States—hoping I'd have this occasion to use it. And everybody seemed to like that touch.

Before heading back to the United States, I wanted to spend three or four days playing some of the other Scottish golf courses I'd been hearing about all my life. There were about five famous ones right in that general area. I didn't get to all of them, but I covered as much ground as I could.

One day I went to Tommy Armour's old club, Lothianburn. There was a tiny item in the papers: BABE TO PLAY TOMMY ARMOUR'S OLD COURSE. And several thousand people showed up there to watch me.

Then I went to Muirfield, where there was such a fog that I could hardly see twenty feet ahead of me, and yet I had one of my best rounds in Scotland. I believe it was a seventy-one. They invited me to have tea afterwards in a beautiful room in the clubhouse. I understand that ordinarily only the men members were allowed in there.

At Glen Eagles I played in a foursome with Jean Donald and Annie Thurban Brown and a man golfer they knew. He was a surgeon. Glen Eagles was more of an American-type course than any I saw over there. They had a beautiful layout with a beautiful hotel.

One club I was determined to see was old St. Andrews. That was a longer trip than the others. We had to start out by taking the ferry over the Firth of Forth, which is where Gullane is located.

It had been announced in the papers that no gallery would be allowed when I played St. Andrews. I wanted a chance to just relax and play the course without a crowd trailing me. Well, they had this railing some distance back of the first tee. When I got there, about a thousand people were jammed behind that railing. I drove off, and none of them moved. I got about a quarter of the way down the fairway, and then I said to myself, "Oh, well." I looked back and waved to them, "Come on!" So those people followed me around the entire eighteen holes.

I had St. Andrews built up in my mind as the most glorious course in the whole world. I'd heard and read so much about it. All the great champions had played there, and it was so rich in tradition.

Well, to tell you the truth, the course gave me an awful letdown. It had been laid out in an era when they didn't hit the ball very far. Traps which they couldn't reach in the old days are right in the way of long drives now. Like most of the Scottish courses that I saw, that St. Andrews layout looked as if a big crane had picked up a lot of dirt and dropped it around and grass had grown there. St. Andrews was just as nature made it. The course had no personality, no contours, no art.

But still it was a thrill for me to be there. When I came up to the last hole, which is probably the most famous hole in the world, I told the gallery how much it meant to me to set foot on it. It carries so many memories of Jones and Hagen and Vardon and Morrissey and the other golf immortals. And I thought of all the great matches that had been decided on that hole, and the hearts that had been broken there.

I went all through Tom Morrissey's old pro shop, and got

176

a big kick out of being presented with a golf club that he used to play with many years ago. Then I visited the golf museum, with its exhibits dating three and four hundred years back—the old-style clubs and the gutta percha balls. I was like a kid looking through a dime store. That museum is a real golf shrine.

I didn't get to play Carnoustie and one or two other courses I'd planned on. I'd already been away from George longer than I ever had been since we got married. I wanted to get back home.

My return trip sure was a contrast to the one coming over. The night before my train left, they had me spend the night at the Ladies' Golf Union building in Edinburgh. At the station when my train pulled out the platform was loaded with people singing "Auld Lang Syne." And two railroad officials were there to see me aboard. They put me in a compartment all by myself. It was loaded with flowers. They served me my tea right there in the compartment.

When I got to London, it was the same thing there. The Ladies' Golf Union put me up for the night, and then I had special accommodations on the boat train to Southampton. And a purser from the boat came to the hotel and took care of my luggage, so I wouldn't have to wait in any lines to get aboard.

The voyage back was real nice. I sailed on the *Queen Elizabeth.* When we were about two hours and forty minutes out of New York, a boat came out to meet us. It was carrying reporters and photographers and newsreel cameramen— seventy-one of them. As their boat got close, I could see a big guy with a white shirt on standing up front at the rail. I said, "That's George!" And it was.

I was hollering and waving to him, and I put two fingers in my mouth and whistled. Just at that moment the whistle on the *Queen Elizabeth* let out a blast. George made a joke out of it later. He said, "Honey, I could hear your whistle above the *Queen Elizabeth*'s."

They let down a rope ladder for these fellows to climb aboard our ship. George was the first to start up it. Our boat gave a little lurch, and I called to him, "Hey, honey, watch out! You're going to turn the *Queen Elizabeth* over!"

When all the press was aboard, it must have taken two hours for the interviewing and picture-taking and what not. I was dressed up in a fancy outfit, but when the cameramen said they wished I was wearing kilts, I told them, "Be right with you," and went and changed. I got a Tartan cap and a pair of kilts for George to pose in, too, and got him to try the Highland Fling.

George and I stayed in New York a couple of days, and our phone seemed to be ringing all the time. One of the newspapermen who called was my great friend Grantland Rice. Granny wasn't very well at that time. He said he'd like to interview me, and George, who took the call, told him, "Sure. We'll come up there." But Granny said that wouldn't be right. He insisted on coming to see us. That's the kind of fellow he always was.

A lot of the calls we got in New York were bids for radio appearances and things like that. But we turned them all down. We also had a visit from our friend Fred Corcoran, the promotion director of the Men's Professional Golf Association. He offered to represent me if I ever did turn pro. We told him that I intended to remain an amateur, but if I should change my mind we'd let him know.

178

Then we went back to Denver, which was my home city at that time. They put on a big celebration for me. They staged a parade through the city streets. They had rigged up a lot of floats, each one representing a different stage in my career—basketball, baseball, javelin-throwing, hurdling and all the rest. I was in the last float, which was stacked with roses. I kept throwing roses to the crowd.

Mayor Quigg Newton and Governor Lee Knous of Colorado were there. At City Hall the Mayor presented me with a giant key to the city. I gave him a big kiss. There was a mob of people watching—about 50,000, according to the newspapers—and they just roared.

The key to the city was about three times as tall as George and weighed 250 pounds. Somebody asked me how I was going to get it home, and I said, "George will carry it." He didn't have to do that, but he did show that he was able to lift it off the ground.

This Denver homecoming was in early July. I was committed to appear in the Broadmoor Match Play Tournament at Colorado Springs in the middle of the month, and I did. I beat Dot Kielty in the finals, ten-and-nine, to stretch my winning streak to seventeen straight. That victory also entitled me to permanent possession of the Broadmoor trophy, which was a big silver cup with a lot of beautiful handwork on it. It had cost them a lot of money. I don't believe they thought anyone would ever retire it. I could see they weren't too happy about having to give it up, so I told them just to make up a plaque for me and keep the cup in competition.

After the Broadmoor tournament I wasn't planning to do much of anything but get ready to defend my American title in the National Women's Amateur in Detroit in September. But in the meantime all sorts of offers kept coming in. It got to the point where I stood to make a fast half-million dollars if I'd turn professional again.

Now George and I didn't need money. He could afford to spend as much as $15,000 a year to pay my expenses on the amateur golf circuit, the way he'd been doing. He had his promotions and a hotel business and other things in Denver. But sometimes offers get so big you feel you just have to take them.

It's pretty hard to say you don't want the kind of money I was being offered. The biggest item was a $300,000 movie deal. A Hollywood official had told George his company would pay me that amount to make a series of ten golf shorts.

It nearly killed me to throw over the amateur standing I'd struggled so hard to get, but I couldn't see any other choice. On August fourteenth we called a press conference in New York, and I announced that I was turning pro. I signed up with Fred Corcoran to be my business representative. He's been representing me ever since, along with his other clients like Ted Williams and Stan Musial.

Well, one of the first things that happened after I went professional again was that the movie deal fell through. It had been a verbal agreement, with nothing in writing. We thought about fighting the case through the courts, but we didn't. Eventually I did make three movie shorts for another studio, Columbia Pictures, although at nowhere near the fabulous price the first people had offered.

But I did cash in on a lot of other things that Fred Corcoran lined up for me. There were lots and lots of exhibition appearances. And I signed up with the Wilson Sporting Goods Company, to be on their advisory staff and have them market Babe Zaharias golf equipment. I'm under a lifetime contract with Wilson now. I also signed with the Serbin dress manufacturers, who make a golf dress that I designed. Then I brought out a golf-instruction book with the firm that is publishing this book, A. S. Barnes and Company.

Fred also booked me into a lot of Sportsmen's Shows, consulting with George on everything, and he arranged special stunts for me like giving golf exhibitions before games in big-league ball parks.

One was Yankee Stadium in New York. I think there were about 60,000 people there that night. I had to stick to demonstrating short stuff. I wanted to take a seven or eight-iron and hit the ball clear over the stadium roof, but they wouldn't let me do it. They were afraid I might miss and injure somebody in the stands.

After I did my golf stuff, I made a pass at playing third base in infield practice. Then I started to pitch. I wanted Joe DiMaggio to come out and swing against me.

I've met Joe several times. He's a great champion. He's a little on the shy side. I went over to the Yankee dugout to get him. "Come on, Joe," I said. "I'm going to pitch to you." He didn't want to come, but I took him by the arm, and I grabbed a bat and handed it to him. I walked Joe out to home plate and bowed low.

All I was afraid of was that I might hit him with a pitch, or that he might hit me with a batted ball. "Whatever you do, please don't line one back at me!" I said to him just before I went to the mound. I did hit him right in the ribs with one pitch, although I don't think it hurt him. But I guess he was being careful about his batting. He skied a few, and then finally he took a big swing and missed and sat down.

I think it was during the spring of that same year that Fred Corcoran arranged a stunt for me with another client of his, Ted Williams, the great baseball star of the Boston Red Sox. Fred had us put on a driving contest in Sarasota, where the Red Sox were training.

Ted is a fine fellow, and, of course, a wonderful athlete. He doesn't especially care for the things that go along with being a champion—the reporters always congregating around, and the autograph collectors, and the people with business propositions. I believe it was because he was getting tired of all this that Ted Williams talked about retiring as early as 1954. It wasn't that he couldn't keep going on the baseball field, because he could.

Ted doesn't get to play too much golf, but he's capable of hitting a golf ball just as hard as he is a baseball. He was rusty and erratic that day on the driving range in Sarasota. When he topped one that just dribbled off the tee, I called to him, "Better run those grounders out, Ted! There may be an overthrow."

During the five minutes or so that we took turns hitting the ball, most of my shots went farther than his did. But I'll have to admit that every so often he whaled one that traveled a longer distance than any tee shot of mine.

What I was doing most of in the months after I turned pro was playing golf exhibitions. The fees were good, but we probably booked too many of them. One month there were seventeen nights that I was on a plane. I'd play in one place, then go to the airport to fly to the next place.

That grind began to wear me down physically, although it was years before I'd admit it. I kept on going at a heavy clip. I'd always felt that no amount of exertion was too much for me, and George was coming to believe that, too. But I found out differently. I'll get to that in a little while.

A schedule packed with other commitments can also dull your tournament sharpness. On October 9, 1947, my streak of seventeen straight championships finally ended in the Texas Women's Open at the River Crest Country Club in Fort Worth. I was playing an eighteen-hole match in the quarterfinals against a young amateur named Bettye Mims White. She got the jump and had me three down after fifteen holes.

I couldn't quite pull out the match. I won the sixteenth and seventeenth with birdies, and had another birdie on the eighteenth, but she got a birdie of her own there by sinking a final six-foot putt after I'd holed mine out. So she beat me one up. Bettye was shooting real good golf that day. She's Mrs. Danoff now, and playing as a professional on our women's circuit.

I bounced back from that defeat and did some more winning. In fact, I set a record in my very next tournament, the Hardscrabble Women's Open at Little Rock, Arkansas. I had a score of 293. That was a world's record then for women in seventy-two holes of tournament medal play.

I honestly believe that if I had squeaked through in the Texas Women's Open, I'd have gone on and stretched my winning streak to twenty-five or thirty tournaments. For a while after that loss a little of my incentive was gone. I didn't have quite so much to work for, now that my string was broken.

As a professional in 1948, I found that there were a few

more tournaments open to me than when I'd first played as a pro back in the 1930's. I even tried to enter the men's National Open, but the United States Golf Association wouldn't let me. They issued a statement, "As the championship has always been intended to be for men, the eligibility rules have been rephrased to confirm that condition. Thus, the USGA has declined an informal entry submitted in behalf of Mrs. George Zaharias."

I don't suppose I'd have finished around the top if they had let me in there. But I don't think I'd have been at the bottom either. I wouldn't have disgraced myself.

In 1948 I did get to play and win both the women's divisions at Tam o' Shanter. I also won the National Women's Open. Then there were several others that I didn't win.

I was very happy about that first National Women's Open victory, although the tournament was still pretty new, and didn't have quite the prestige that it does today. It was played at the Atlantic City Country Club. I went right into the lead and stayed there all the way. I took the $1200 first prize by a margin of eight strokes with a 300 score.

An additional prize of $1000 was offered to anyone who could break 300. If I'd sunk a five-foot putt on the last hole, I'd have got that too. "Oh, well," I said, when my putt just missed dropping, "I'd only have had to give the money to the government for income taxes."

It wasn't my tournament earnings that had me in a high income bracket that year. It was all the other things I was doing on the side. I was the leading women's money winner for 1948, and my winnings totaled just $3400. As you can see by that, the amount of competition available to a woman golf pro was still pretty limited.

That was the one fly in the ointment for me. George realized this, and he started thinking about the problem, the way he had been when I was up against the same situation during my earlier pro period. And once again George came up with an answer. He got the idea that there should be a professional tournament circuit for women, just as there was for men.

CHAPTER 15

When George set out to get the ball rolling for a women's pro golf tour late in 1948, he had himself an uphill roll. One big problem was that there were so few women golf professionals. In addition to myself, there was only Patty Berg, Helen Dettweiler, Betty Jameson, Betty Hicks, Bea Gottlieb and one or two others. Patty Berg was about the only one who was really active. Like me, she was working for the Wilson Sporting Goods Company, and giving exhibitions all over the country.

But George talked up the idea with people like L. B. Icely, the president of the Wilson company, and Fred Corcoran, who'd had many years of experience with the men's tour. George persuaded them that once we got the thing going, it would build itself up. Mr. Icely agreed to put some Wilson money behind a women's circuit, and Fred agreed to organize it.

In January of 1949, George and Fred and I had a meeting at the Venetian Hotel in Miami with Patty Berg. We formed the Ladies' Professional Golf Association. There had previously been a Women's Professional Golfers Association, headed by Hope Seignious. We called her up and invited her to be president of our new association. She had been ill, and said she wouldn't be able to take on the job, but she wished us luck. So Patty Berg became president of the Ladies' PGA for the first year. I've been president since.

Things went along pretty slowly at the start, but eventually it started to snowball, both in number of tournaments and number of players. At first we'd play for anything we could get. The total purses for 1949 didn't come to more than $15,000. By 1955 the minimum per tournament was $5000, and the total prize money for the year was around $200,000.

Meanwhile I kept on making plenty of money from non-tournament stuff. And I was working hard for it. To give you one example, there was a weekend in June of 1948 when I started out playing in New Canaan, Connecticut. Then we got in the car and drove to Detroit to play there on a Sunday. And from Detroit we went right on to Chicago for the Western Women's Open that coming week.

I got to the finals against Patty Berg. We were all square at the end of thirty-six holes. And I had to catch a plane that night to fly back to Connecticut and play there on Monday. I could see circling overhead the little chartered plane that was going to take me from the golf course to make my airline connection. It happened to be my birthday, June twenty-sixth. I got a big cake on the first tee, but I didn't get the championship trophy. Patty Berg outlasted me to win on the thirty-seventh hole, one up.

I became a playing pro from Grossinger's in New York around that time. Then in October of 1950 I was invited by Eugene Dyer, the owner of the Sky Crest Country Club outside Chicago, to serve as their teaching pro. I was the first woman ever to hold that job at a swank club. I was tickled to accept the offer, because it was such a boost for women's standing in the golf world. My contract guaranteed me a minimum of $20,000 a year at Sky Crest, and also allowed me to play outside tournaments and exhibitions. They had a little private airfield right there at the club to make traveling easier—this was the same course where that airplane had been circling when I lost the 1948 Western Women's Open to Patty Berg.

I put in a lot of long hours giving lessons. It was hard work, but I loved it. We moved from Denver to Sky Crest, and had a nice place out there at the club. We were really living high off the hog.

One night George said, "Come on and get dressed. I'm taking you in town to dinner tonight."

We often drove into Chicago for dinner like that. I was pretty tired from a day of teaching golf, but I put on my new girdle and one of my best new dresses and got myself all dolled up for dining and dancing or whatever George had in mind.

We started off in the car, and came into the outskirts of Chicago. George stopped the car at a diner. I thought he probably knew the proprietor or something, and wanted to

188

talk to him for a minute. I was going to wait in the car, but George said, "Come on in."

So I went inside with him, and George pointed to two stools and said, "Let's take these." Now I supposed his idea was to have a cup of coffee before we went on downtown to dinner. But when the waitress came over, George ordered two hamburgers, two bowls of chili, and two glasses of buttermilk.

That's what I used to practically live on in my early years as a golfer, and I still order it often when I'm on the road. But we'd been eating hardly anything but choice steaks and stuff since we came to Sky Crest.

I said to George, "Say, what is all this?"

He said, "I just didn't want you to get out of the habit." So we ate our hamburgers and chili, and drank our buttermilk. And then we drove back home to the Sky Crest Country Club.

That club changed hands in 1951, and then later on that year George and I bought our own golf course—the old Forest Hills Country Club in Tampa, Florida. We made some changes and improvements, and renamed it the Tampa Golf and Country Club, and built up the membership to 375.

But all this while something else was happening. It started in 1948. I traveled out to an award-presentation affair for honor caddies. A number of big-name people were there —Bing Crosby, Bob Hope, Jimmy Demaret, Frank Stranahan, Louise Suggs, Patty Berg. Coming home on a plane, I suddenly had this terrific pain in my left side. There was a big swelling there. Then the pain stopped after a while, and the swelling went down.

It went on like that for several years. This pain and swelling would come, and then it would go. I'd say to myself, "I

189

should see a doctor about this, but I'm too busy right now. I'll have to put it off for a while."

A little rest always seemed to fix me up. A good hot bath, and a good night's sleep, and I'd be ready to go again. I kept on playing, and did my share of winning. In 1949 I was first again in prize money. The total only came to $4300—our Ladies' PGA was just getting underway. My tournament victories included the Tam o' Shanter "World Championship" and the Eastern Women's Open. I was second to Louise Suggs in the National Women's Open.

In 1950 I had a real good year. I won just about all the top tournaments—both the "All-American" and the "World" at Tam o' Shanter, the National Women's Open at Wichita, the Women's Titleholders at Augusta and the Western Women's Open at Denver. I was on top in money-winnings again, this time with $13,550.

In 1951 I scored another double at Tam o' Shanter, which helped put me at the head of the money list once more. The total this time was $15,087. When I didn't win a tournament, I'd almost always be second or third, or no worse than fourth or fifth. Nobody can be first in all of them, of course, with the competition as tough as it is in women's golf today.

I started off as if I was going to have the same sort of year in 1952. I was up around the top in every tournament I played. I won the Women's Titleholders in March, and I took the first two legs of the Weathervane. That was a tournament where we played thirty-six holes in each of four different cities. The one with the lowest aggregate score would win.

Again I was the leading women's money-winner as we came to the end of April. But now that trouble in my left side was really getting to me. The pain and the swelling came more often. They were more severe, and I couldn't seem to shake off the attacks as fast as I had before.

We went out to the West Coast for the last tournament in April, the Richmond Women's Open at Richmond, California. In the final round I faded off to a seventy-seven and wound up in fifth place. George was with me, and he was getting worried. He thought I should take some time off and find out what was wrong, but I felt it was my duty to continue with the tour as long as I was able. I kept a date to play in Bakersfield, and then in Fresno.

We moved up the West Coast for the third leg of the Weathervane at Seattle. This was in May. Well, those thirty-six holes were just agony for me. I finished eleventh, which was the worst I'd ever done in a medal-play tournament. George urged me to drop out after the first eighteen holes, but somehow I got around the course the last day. And I was really dragging.

I hoped that rest would straighten me out again, but after a day or two I gave up. The pain was so bad now that I couldn't stand it any longer. I told George, "I think I'd better go to a hospital." He said, "I think so too."

I wanted to be treated by my family doctor in Beaumont, Texas. That's Dr. W. E. Tatum, a wonderful man. So I phoned him and then went by plane to Beaumont. They were ready for me there. I was admitted right away to the Hotel Dieu Hospital.

Well, what I'd had all this time was a hernia at the top of my left thigh—a femoral hernia. It was in the strangulated stage now. Doctor Tatum told me that if I'd let it go another week I might have been a goner. That was on a Friday. It was Monday before he could operate. They had to build me up first. I was in an anemic condition, I suppose from over-exertion and fatigue.

The operation came off fine. I went back to our home, which was now at the Tampa Golf & Country Club, and began picking up right away. It would be a while before my operation mended enough for me to go back to the golf tournaments, but I chipped and putted a little.

Although I couldn't play in the National Women's Open, which was being held at the Bala Golf Club in Philadelphia the last week in June, I was invited up there to act as starter. So I went, and sat on the starter's bench at the first tee. The opening day I said, "I'm going to hit the first ball." I didn't risk swinging a driver. I took something like a three-iron and smacked that ball out there 180 or 190 yards. And that was as long as most of the drives that were made off that tee the first day.

After the Open I continued to work myself back into condition in Tampa. I kept phoning Doctor Tatum and asking him when it would be all right for me to enter a tournament again. I was hoping to compete in the "All-American" and the "World Championship" at Tam o' Shanter in August.

Doctor Tatum said he'd give me the word when it was okay for me to get back in action again. That smart doctor of mine! When the first day of the "All-American" was over he phoned me and said, "Well, Babe, it's all right for you to go up to Chicago now."

I said, "Why didn't you tell me last week, so I could have gone up there and played in both the 'All-American' and the 'World'?"

He said, "Because I didn't want you to play in both of them."

192

I did get to Tam o' Shanter in time to enter the "World." They'd taken to calling this tournament "the Babe Zaharias benefit," because I'd won it all the four times it had been held. Well, for a while there in 1952 it seemed that I might make it five in a row. I had a pretty good round the first day, and also the second day. Then I began to tire. I did all right the third day on the outgoing nine holes, but tailed off coming back. The fourth day it was the same. I had a good chance to win after nine holes, then I ran out of gas again, and wound up third behind Betty Jameson and Patty Berg.

Back home in Tampa I practiced some more, and kept feeling better. The Texas Women's Open that October was being held at the River Crest Country Club in Fort Worth. It's a short course. I had never done much good there. It's small and narrow, with about fourteen places where you can go out of bounds. River Crest was where my record streak of seventeen straight tournaments got broken back in the fall of 1947. That course had whipped me just about every time I'd competed there.

I said to George, "I'm going to go down and beat that golf course." So I went there about a week ahead and practiced. I did whip the course, and I won the tournament. I felt wonderful.

Then I came back to Tampa, and before long I wasn't feeling wonderful any more. November and December are the months when the tournament circuit closes down, and you figure on taking it easy and getting your pep back. But it wasn't working that way for me this time. I wasn't in pain, the way I had been before my hernia operation. Oh, there were some little symptoms. But mostly the thing was that I seemed to be tired all the time. When I played a round of golf, I never felt like I wanted to play another nine holes, which I generally did in the past.

In January I came back as usual for the 1953 tournament circuit. I wasn't winning much of anything. Half the time I wasn't even finishing in the first five. I'd shoot a good round, or a good nine holes, and then I'd tire. Those wonderful rub-downs that George gave me never seemed to reach quite deep enough any more to get all the tiredness out of my muscles.

On March ninth in Florida I placed second to Patty Berg in the Jacksonville Women's Open. The next week I dropped down to sixth place in the Women's Titleholders. I was feeling worse and worse. George was getting more and more worried. He was with me the week after that during the Peach Blossom-Betsy Rawls tournament in Spartanburg, South Carolina. I just about made it through the last eighteen holes, and finished completely out of the running.

George made a doctor's appointment for me right then and there in Spartanburg. I talked him out of it. "I'll be all right once I get a good night's sleep," I said. "In another couple of weeks the tour will hit Beaumont. Then I'll see Doctor Tatum again and have him give me a check-up."

During the next few days both my health and my golf game did seem to perk up some. On March thirtieth, when we teed for the final round of the New Orleans Women's Open, I was only one stroke behind Patty Berg. The best I could do was a seventy-nine, and she wound up winning the tourna-ment by four strokes. But at least I was able to hold onto second place.

Then we went to Beaumont. I was really determined to make a good showing there, because this was my hometown, and the tournament had been created in my honor—the

194

Babe Zaharias Open. I ran into Doctor Tatum out at the Beaumont Country Club before the competition started, and told him I wanted a check-up when it was over. He suggested an appointment a couple of days after the end of the tournament, and I said, "I can't wait that long. I have to go on from here to the next tournament in Phoenix." So he said to come and see him the morning after the final round.

I'll never know where I got the energy to play that tournament. It was three rounds of medal play instead of the regular four rounds, which was a good thing for me. I doubt that I could have played a fourth day.

Well, the first two days I put together about the best pair of rounds I'd shot on the whole winter tour. I took the lead with 142—two strokes under par—and I practically exhausted myself doing it. I was only one stroke ahead of Louise Suggs at that point, though, and there were several others who were close enough to have a chance.

The last day it was more of an effort to play than ever. I wasn't in command of my shots the way I'd been the first two rounds. I lost three strokes to par on the outgoing nine. By the time we reached the sixteenth I was four strokes over. Then I was able to birdie the sixteenth and get one of those strokes back.

My buddy, Betty Dodd, a girl I encouraged to go into professional golf, had completed her own round and come out to root me home. She knew that Louise Suggs had finished with a 218 total, and Patty Berg with a 219. But I didn't know it.

I saw Betty Dodd standing there when I came off the sixteenth green. I asked her, "How do I stand with the field?" Some golfers don't like to be told. It makes them choke up.

But I always feel that I play better when I know what I have to do.

Betty told me, "All you've got to do is get two pars to win." That would give me a final score of 217.

Well, I missed my par on the seventeenth hole. I knocked the ball up on the green about twelve feet from the cup, and then I went and three-putted. I hit my first putt about four feet beyond the hole, and missed again coming back.

Now I needed a par on the eighteenth to tie for first place —or a birdie to win. The eighteenth was a par four hole. I felt as though I was crawling on my hands and knees by now. I got up there on the tee and pulled myself together and slugged that ball with all my might. And I hooked it over behind a tree.

One more bad shot, and I was going to blow this tournament. But I managed to come up with one more good shot. I took an iron and carried that ball onto the green about six feet from the pin. Then I knocked in my putt for the birdie I needed to win.

That hometown gallery went wild. Betty Dodd and Patty Berg and some of the other girls rushed onto the green and lifted me up in the air. They practically carried me off to the clubhouse. Television cameras were going and everything.

I should have been in a mood for celebrating, but I wasn't. As soon as I could get away I went right up to my room and stretched out on the bed. I'd never felt so completely played out.

This was on a Sunday night. On Monday morning I had that appointment with Doctor Tatum. After I finished with that, George and I were going to take off in the car.

I began packing for both of us Monday morning, the

way I'd always been in the habit of doing. But I was still fagged out. Even packing seemed too much of an effort. I said to George, "Honey, will you finish the job while I run down to see Doctor Tatum?"

A short time later I was in Doctor Tatum's office. He had me get up on the examination table. He checked on the operation I'd had the year before, and said, "Well, everything seems to be all right."

Then he probed around some more. I could see his face out of the corner of my eye. All of a sudden he just turned white.

He didn't say a word. I guess I'd suspected all along what my trouble was. I said to him, "I've got cancer, haven't I?"

CHAPTER 16

I've never been one to worry much about my health, but I'd been feeling so low for several months in 1953 that I couldn't help thinking once in a while that I just might have cancer. I was pretty sure of it from the way Doctor Tatum suddenly went white while he was examining me.

But when I asked him straight out if I had cancer, he said, "Now, Babe, we don't know that. But here's what I want you to do. I want you to go to Fort Worth and see a specialist there, a proctologist, and have him make some tests."

I said, "Can't I see him when I come back this way to play in the Texas Women's Open in October?"

He said, "No, you'll have to go down there today. I'll phone ahead and make the arrangements."

This was on a Monday morning, April sixth. George and I had planned to go from Beaumont to San Antonio, where Betty Dodd lived with her family. We were going to spend the night there, and then caravan it with Betty to Phoenix in time for the start of the Phoenix Women's Open on Thursday.

I came back from Doctor Tatum's office and told George that we'd have to change our plans and go to Fort Worth, because I was supposed to see a specialist there. We set off in the car, and got to the specialist's office in Fort Worth in the early evening.

He was Dr. William C. Tatum—no relation to the Doctor Tatum in Beaumont. He did what they call taking some biopsies for analysis. He said he'd have the results for us at eleven o'clock Wednesday morning.

We waited it out at the home of R. L. and Bertha Bowen, the close friends we always visit when we're in Fort Worth. I phoned Betty Dodd at her home in San Antonio, and explained why I'd had to come to Fort Worth and wouldn't be able to make the Phoenix Open after all. I said, "Why don't you come over for a visit?"—she'd become good friends with the Bowens too—and Betty decided she would.

Once on the circuit when I was all fagged out I'd let the remark slip to Betty, "Maybe I have cancer." I'd said it in a joking way, but it was enough to get her worried. I'd never even hinted at such a thing to George, and as we sweated it out there in Fort Worth, I continued to keep my cancer fears a secret from him.

It turned out that toward the end George was doing the

199

same thing with me. Dr. William C. Tatum took those biopsies on Monday evening, and we wouldn't have the verdict until Wednesday. So George thought he might as well go down to the doctor's office on Tuesday and get a routine check-up for himself.

The doctor looked him over and told him he was all right, and then George asked, "How about my wife?"

And the doctor said, "I'm afraid she has cancer."

Right after that George telephoned me at the Bowens. "Honey," he says, "while I'm downtown I think I'll see a couple of movies. You know how I always like to go to picture shows, and you don't. I'll get myself a bite for supper, and see you later in the evening."

I didn't find it out until long after, but George was so upset by what the doctor had told him that he wanted time to pull himself together before he came back and faced me. George went to about three picture shows in a row, hardly noticing what was on the screen. He finally got back to the house a little before bedtime.

We turned in, and I just couldn't get to sleep. Once in a while I'd light a cigarette. Finally George sat up and said, "You're not sleeping."

I said, "Yes, and neither are you."

George went to the kitchen and made us a pot of coffee. We talked for a while, and then we did get to sleep. We woke up in plenty of time to make our eleven o'clock appointment with Dr. William C. Tatum.

We got to his reception room right on the dot, and his wife, who acted as his secretary, took us in to see him, and seated us side by side.

The doctor didn't do any hemming or hawing. "Babe," he

200

said, "you've got cancer." I thought I was prepared for it, but that report just hit me like a thunderbolt. George too. His hand shot out and grabbed mine.

The doctor went straight on talking, I suppose to get us started right in thinking about what could be done. He said my cancer was in the rectum, and that I needed a colostomy. He brought out pictures and diagrams to show us what kind of operation that was—how they'd cut off part of the lower intestine, and reroute it, and make a new outlet in the left side of the abdomen.

I guess he talked to us there for about two hours. He told me I'd be able to play golf again after the operation, although probably not tournament golf. He said to go ahead and get other medical opinions if we wanted.

We left his office, and I was crying when we went down on the elevator. George was all distressed. He had never seen me cry before, and I don't believe he saw me do it any more after that. We got back to Bowens, and I told Bertha the news, and she just flew up in the air. She started bawling, and phoned her husband, "R. L., come home quick! The worst has happened!"

I went off by myself for a while and lay on a bed, thinking, "What in the world have I done wrong in my life to deserve this?" I'd always tried to do right, and help other people. I'd played in I don't know how many benefits for the American Cancer Society. I kept saying to myself, "God, why did I have to have this? Why does anybody have to have it?" But my idea has always been that whatever God intended for me in this life, I'd go along with.

George and all the rest of them were out there crying. Finally George settled down long enough to call Doctor

Tatum in Beaumont, and Doctor Tatum said to come on back there. We decided to stop overnight on the way with my brother Louis and his wife Thelma in Newton, Texas—they have an electrical business there.

We got ready to leave the Bowens. It didn't take much preparation, because we'd hardly unpacked the car at all since we got there. I get plenty of golf supplies, since I'm under contract to a sporting-goods company, and every time we visited the Bowens, I used to give R. L. some of my practice balls.

This time when we got out to the car, I saw my golf clubs sitting in it, and that was one of the few moments I let myself give in to despair. I grabbed the bag and handed it to R. L. and said, "Here! I want you to have these, because I won't be needing them any more."

George snatched the bag and said, "No, honey, no! You'll play again!"

We had a nightmare trip 280 miles to my brother's house in Newton. George was driving, and he had to stop the car at times because he couldn't see through his tears. George is very sentimental. You can touch him easy. I can say the wrong thing to George sometimes, not thinking, and he'll feel bad about it.

We talked and we planned. I was thinking about my golf clubs, and my cocker spaniels. I was thinking about George more than anything else, of course. And I was thinking about my sisters and brothers and my good friends—all the people I'd have to leave if this cancer had gone too far. The one thing that made me feel a little better was that Doctor Tatum in Fort Worth had said, "You have caught your cancer very early." I had No. 3 type. No. 4 is the fastest growing, and No. 3 is next, and No. 2 and No. 1 are not so severe.

So we got to my brother's house, and there were more tears. Louis broke down. He and I had always been so close, ever since we were youngsters. He kept saying, "Babe did nothing but good. Why couldn't this have happened to me, or to somebody else beside her?"

Louis and Thelma got their family doctor, Dr. Whitecloud, to come over. He talked to me about what a colostomy was, and gave me all the best answers to boost my morale. Then he had George and me take some sleeping pills, so we'd get a good night's rest.

We went on the next morning to Beaumont. Somehow a rumor had already leaked out of Fort Worth that I had cancer, and the press was waiting for us outside Doctor Tatum's office. I went on into the office. George fended off the reporters for a while and then came in too. Both of us always believe in co-operating with the press, but naturally George didn't feel like giving out the cancer story just then.

Doctor Tatum put me right into the Hotel Dieu, the hospital where I'd had my hernia operation the year before. I wanted my same room back, No. 201, and they were able to give it to me after a couple of days. That's a Catholic hospital. I'm not a Catholic myself, but Sister Mary Daniels and the other nuns were just wonderful to me both times I was in there. I couldn't have asked for finer treatment.

Meanwhile we'd gotten in touch with Betty Dodd and given her the news. She'd missed connections with us in Fort Worth—she'd been in an auto accident on her way there— but I finally got hold of her on the phone and said, "Well,

Betty, I've got cancer. I have to have a 'costomy' or something like that." I couldn't even pronounce the word yet.

Betty said, "You mean a colostomy! I know what that is. I know a woman who has one."

Betty is a Texas girl, the daughter of a retired Army general. She's a fine young golfer. I first got to know her when she was playing the golf circuit as an amateur in 1950. I worked with her some, the way veteran golfers used to work with me when I was starting out. Eventually I helped get her started as a professional. She's like a daughter to me. George and I see a lot of her both on the circuit and during the off season. Sometimes she gets out her guitar, and I get my harmonica, and we play some of that real Southern-style music.

Well, Betty went on in to Fort Worth to see the Bowens, and then came up to Beaumont. George had a business deal hanging fire in Denver. He was negotiating the sale of the hotel he owned there. At the hospital they weren't going to do anything with me for a few days but take x-rays and stuff. I told George to go ahead and make a quick run out to Denver, now that Betty was on hand to keep me company. Betty got them to put a cot right in my room for her. She stayed there all the way through.

The first thing that happened when I got in the hospital, Sister Daniels walked into the room to greet me and said, "Here's a hospital cocktail for you." It was castor oil! I hadn't taken that since I was a kid. But I needed stuff like that to get me in shape for the x-rays. During one stretch of twenty-four hours they were x-raying me from head to foot. I couldn't have any food or anything during that time.

George had told Doctor Tatum, "Get Babe the finest

204

surgeon. I don't care what it costs. Anything to get her well."

And Doctor Tatum had said, "George, we don't have to go very far to find the right man. We've got him down here in Galveston, at the John Sealy Hospital of the University of Texas medical school."

That was Dr. Robert Moore. He agreed to do the operation. The first time he came to see me in my room, he put out his hand and said, "Babe, I certainly hate to meet you under these circumstances."

I said, "Doctor Moore, under these circumstances I'm tickled pink to meet you! I know I've got the best."

A couple of days after I entered the hospital, the story was out in the newspapers that I was going to be operated on for what they called "a serious malignancy." About this time George left on his Denver trip, and the impression got around that he was scouring the country for a surgeon to perform the operation. Some important friends of ours called George up and offered to help. One of them was Walter Winchell, who has made a specialty of the fight against cancer. But when George told him that we already had Doctor Moore lined up, Walter Winchell said that we couldn't have found a better man for the job. Then he wired me at the hospital:

JUST SPOKE TO GEORGE ON THE PHONE AND I WANTED TO LET YOU KNOW HOW UNHAPPY I AM OVER YOUR ILLNESS BUT BABE YOU ARE GOING TO BE OKAY BECAUSE THE MEN IN CHARGE OF YOU ARE THE VERY BEST I HAVE NEVER FORGOTTEN HOW MUCH YOU DID TO HELP SO MANY OTHER STRICKEN PEOPLE THROUGH THE RUNYON FUND.

Telegrams were coming in from all over. There was a wire from Augusta, Georgia, where the Masters Tournament was going on, reading, BEST OF LUCK AND LOVE FROM YOUR SWEETHEARTS IN THE PRESS STY. It had forty-one names signed to it. There was one signed, THE BOYS FROM THE PHILA PHILLIES, and another with the signature, LOU BOUDREAU, BILL MCKECHNIE, DEL BAKER AND THE BOSTON RED SOX.

I heard from Bobby Jones and Ed Sullivan and Fred Waring. Pepper Martin wired me, and Clark Griffith, and Del Webb. There were so many wonderful people who sent me messages of encouragement—men and women both in and out of the sports world. Those messages were all equally appreciated, and I just wish I had space to list every one of them.

The telephone was banging away too. Bob Hope called, and Grantland Rice, and Mickey Rooney. There'd be one party on the line, and a couple more waiting to get on.

The room filled up with flowers until I told the nuns to give them to patients that didn't have any. And the mail kept building up. First they were bringing me letters by the handful. Then they brought it in a basket. Finally they had to use a big wicker clothes hamper to carry in all the mail.

Betty or George would open the letters as they came in. I read a lot of them myself before surgery. But eventually the mail got ahead of us. Some of it was from overseas. I must have received about 20,000 letters from the public while I was in there. I haven't been able to acknowledge them all to this day, although I did ask the press to thank the people for me. It really bucked me up to know that I had so many folks all over the world pulling for me.

Some were well-meaning people who told me not to get operated on. They had "cures" they wanted me to take instead. Go here, go there, go to this person. Take the grape diet. I got herbs from South Africa. From Australia they wanted to send me herbs. I got holy water, and every kind of thing you can imagine.

An occasional person wasn't satisfied just to write me a letter. One night I walked out of my room to get a little exercise, and a woman practically pounced on me in the corridor. She was a stranger who had come into the hospital looking for me. She gave me a long harangue about how God had sent her to save me, and now my cancer would be cured without any operation. She was very sincere about it.

One man called me on the phone and began talking about how the mineral springs at Mineral Wells, Texas, would fix me up. He wanted to come and tell me about it. I finally turned the phone over to Betty Dodd, and after a few more minutes she convinced him that no callers were being admitted to my room.

My sister Lillie was with us at the time. She lives in Beaumont—she's Mrs. O. B. Grimes. When she got home that night, here was this same fellow camped at her house. He was an Indian—a great huge fellow, Lillie told us later. She was scared to death. Since he couldn't get in to see me at the hospital, he'd come to try and sell Babe's sister on the mineral springs idea. It was quite a while before Lillie could get rid of him.

Lillie was at the hospital constantly. All my brothers and sisters were there. I'm mighty fond and proud of each one of them. They're all married and have children. I've told you about Lillie in Beaumont, and my brother Louis in Newton, Texas, and my sister Dora out in Arizona. Esther Nancy is Mrs. Philip Koth now. She lives in Santa Monica, California, where her husband is president of a gas company. My brother Ole is still in Texas, and so is my youngest brother, Arthur, who lives in Baytown.

Well, the doctors spent several days there on the x-rays and tests, and found out that my cancer was localized. There was no trace of it anywhere else in my body. In a cancer case that's good news, but I couldn't do too much cheering, because I still didn't like the idea of a colostomy. I didn't want my body changed permanently like that. Sometimes they can perform a temporary operation instead, and then resect and reconnect the intestine later. I kept hoping they could do that with my cancer.

But I knew that whichever way it worked out, the operation had to be done. In a room across the hall from me there was another patient who didn't want a colostomy, a nun called Sister Tarsisis. I believe that's how the name is spelled. She'd been there a year and a half, and wasted away to almost nothing, and she was still refusing to have the operation. They had me talk to her, and George too. They thought it might help her to know somebody who was going through with it. And she was getting to where she was willing to consider surgery.

After they finished with the x-rays, they were another few days putting me in shape for surgery. I was getting a lot of pills. I wasn't eating anything at all, because they had to have the intestines clear when they operated. They were feeding me through the veins. It was good having Betty in the room with me at night, so I could talk to someone when I felt like it, because I sure wasn't doing much sleeping.

Then the day came. It was Friday, April seventeenth. That afternoon I was going into the operating room.

CHAPTER 17

The morning of April seventeenth, they began coming in and giving me preliminary shots and everything to get me ready for surgery in the afternoon. Sister Daniels told me that the nuns were going to have a novena that day and pray for a successful operation—and no permanent colostomy. Betty Dodd went in the chapel for a novena herself.

Everybody was encouraging me. I said, "Don't worry. I'm all right. I'll just leave everything in the hands of God."

I had been to God, I guess, more than I ever had before in my life. I have never been what you'd call a real church-going Christian, but I've always said my prayers that I learned when I was a little kid, and I still say the same prayers today.

209

But when you get sick, God is the one you go to. He gives you the spiritual muscle that you need.

One of the last things I did before the operation was to tell George, "Honey, I want you to go downstairs and get my golf clubs and put them right in the corner of my room, because I'm going to use them again. I want to look at them and I want to feel that they're there when I come out of the operating room." So he did, and those clubs stayed in that corner as long as I was in the hospital.

I was supposed to go up to surgery at one o'clock, but there was some hold-up there, so it was around two o'clock when they wheeled me out of my room. Sister Tarsisis across the way had asked to be allowed to see me before I left, so I had them stop at her doorway. I waved to her and called, "Sister Tarsisis, I'm going up now. I'll be seeing you in a little while."

George went up in the elevator with me to the fourth floor, where surgery was. There were reporters and photographers waiting in the corridor. George said, "Don't take any pictures *now!*"

I said, "All right, honey, we don't have to have any pictures." But I raised myself up. Bill Scurlock was there—Tiny Scurlock. He's a Beaumont sportswriter. He's known me since I was a kid in school. He asked me if I had any statement I wanted to make, and I said, "Tiny, tell everybody to pray double hard for me, and I'll be back. And tell people to give their money to the Cancer Fund instead of sending me flowers."

George leaned down and gave me a last little pep talk and a kiss. Then they wheeled me into surgery. They were going to lift me onto the operating table, but I told them, "I'll get on the table myself."

There must have been ten or twelve people there—doctors and nurses and so forth. I could hear them talking, and sense people moving around. Doctor Moore came in. He said, "It's going to be a tough round today." He was always talking to me like that. I said, "Yeah, but maybe we'll make a few putts."

He told me, "You've got to do one more thing for me. You've got to swallow this tube for me." And I did. Then one of the nuns doubled me up so they could give me a spinal anesthetic. I could hear the doctors talking faintly for a moment, and then I didn't know another thing.

They had to do a permanent colostomy. I was on the table almost four hours. I opened my eyes coming back down in the elevator. They'd given me some transfusions to keep my strength up during the operation. When the elevator doors opened, George rushed up and took charge of the last bottle of blood.

I said, "Colostomy, honey?"

He said, "Yes. It's all right." Then I closed my eyes and went to sleep again.

Most of what I know about the next fourteen or fifteen days is things George and Betty told me later. I was only half-conscious the first five or six days. There was a tube down my nose and needles in my arms. And they kept giving me shots because I had so much pain.

The first twenty-four hours after a major operation they keep turning you in bed, so the blood will circulate freely and no clots will form. I had two night nurses, and Betty

Dodd was there to help them, but it's not easy to move dead weight. And they didn't want to jerk me around too hard.

Betty thought she'd try something to make the turning easier on me and everybody else. I seemed to be unconscious, but she leaned down and said, "Come on, Babe, raise yourself up a bit."

Betty says that I arched up like a cat on my shoulders and feet, so that she had to tell me, "For crying out loud, not that far! You'll wreck all the stitches."

Sometimes I'd start to jerk my arms, and the needles that were stuck in there for the intravenous feeding would come out. But Betty found she could stop that by grabbing my hand and telling me not to pull. She says that eventually all she had to do was just touch my finger.

I didn't know exactly where I was or what I was saying. I'd think I was smoking, and I'd say, "Would you put this out?" They'd say, "Put what out?", and I'd answer, "Put out this cigarette for me."

Or I'd be telling everybody to be quiet. I thought I was back in the auditorium in school. No talking was allowed there.

Everything was pretty much of a blur for a while, but I do remember that the tube down my nose kept bothering me. It went all the way down to my stomach, but I thought it was just stuck in my throat. My throat felt raw and blistered. I couldn't swallow. To relieve the discomfort, I'd lift that tube out a little and prop it against my nose. Then when I fell asleep it would drop back and hit me in the same place again.

About the fifth or sixth day Doctor Moore came in and

said, "We're going to fix you up today." He meant that they were going to cauterize me where I'd had the colostomy.

I said, "Are you going to take this tube out of my nose, too?" He said, "Yes, we'll take that out." The cauterizing was no fun, but it sure was a relief to get rid of that tube.

I wasn't sleeping well at night, even with all the drugs and pain-killers they were giving me. After I had breakfast in the morning, and they gave me my bath, then I could really sleep for a while.

George told me that one day he was in the room while I was dozing, and I began playing golf in my sleep. He says he knew it by the way I was moving my hands and my feet, and twisting my head back and forth. When I finally opened my eyes, he said, "Did you have a nice round, honey? I saw you hit that last drive."

I think it was the day after the tube came out of my nose that they wanted me to get up and try to walk, which of course they have you do very early after operations nowadays. And I couldn't even sit up. But they propped me on the edge of the bed, and set me on my feet. I tried to take a step—and then they had to catch me before I fell. The next time it was a little better, though, and it got better each time after that.

Lying in bed, I'd keep looking at those golf clubs in the corner. Then I'd look at my arms, and look at my legs. They were nothing but bone. I'd lost a lot of weight, and it was mostly muscle weight. I said to myself, "If I can exercise my arms and legs while I'm here in bed, then I'll probably come along faster when I'm on my feet again."

So I started raising one leg up in the air, and then the other. I was working my muscles and pushing them—working my arms and my legs. One of those early days I got out of bed by myself and walked over to the golf clubs. I picked out a four wood and took my grip on it. And it felt real good. Then I went out in the hall with my golf club, but I felt a little weak at this point, so I got back in bed.

They were having a party one day for graduating nurses. Sister Daniels asked Betty to come with her guitar and me with my harmonica. I went as far as the door to the party, and then they had to escort me back to my room.

But I was getting stronger all the time. Along around the fifteenth or sixteenth day, I said it would be all right for the newsreel and television men to come in with their cameras. They were there three or four hours with those floodlights. I still wasn't on my feet very much at this stage, so I posed in bed for them. I was setting my hair, after just having washed it. I knew that it would encourage other cancer patients if they saw me getting well. I wanted the public to know I was all right.

I got to where I was taking walks in the corridors. All the time I was walking I was doing exercises with my arms and my legs. Then Sister Daniels said to me, "Babe, let's go visit some of the other patients. They want to meet you." We covered just about that whole hospital before I left.

I started getting out of the hospital to ride in the automobile with George and Betty. We took real short drives at first, and then longer ones. The hospital was on the Gulf shore, and I began sitting out for an hour at a time to watch the boat races.

Another thing that happened, Sister Tarsisis went through with her colostomy. She was able to have hers resected and reconnected later on. I saw her a couple of years

214

afterward, and she was doing fine. Her weight was up to normal, and she was back on the job again.

There was one last thing. After helping to nurse me for weeks, what should Betty Dodd do but come down with a hernia attack like the one I'd had the year before. They persuaded her to get it fixed up right away, and she had an operation. So my last week in the hospital, she was the new patient in our room, and I was helping her out a little bit.

My brother Louis and his wife Thelma had told me that when I got out of the hospital, they wanted me to come to their place in Newton to convalesce. They invited George and Betty, too. On May twenty-second, forty-three days from the time I went into the hospital, I was discharged. I was saying good-by to all the sisters. A lot of them were crying, and I was sort of wet-eyed myself.

Louis and Thelma had their automobile waiting outside the hospital. They'd rigged up a bed in the back of the car for me, and I lay there all the way to Newton. We got to the house, and the television cameramen showed up again.

Louis and Thelma wanted to fatten me up. What spreads they put on—meat balls, corn bread, black-eyed peas, string beans. But even with the enormous meals they served, I couldn't seem to gain any weight at first. Later on I was sorry that I'd tried so hard to put the weight on. I not only gained back what I'd lost, but went ten pounds over.

I just took it easy at my brother's house. I'd go out in the back yard and sit, and then I'd come in and lie down. It tires you to sit very long when you first come out of the hospital. I was knitting socks and everything, but I wanted something else to do. A friend of mine sent me a painting set, so I went out in the back yard and started to paint. I said, "I'm going to be like Grandma Moses, or Ike." I got one pretty nice scene down on canvas, although I didn't have enough time to really finish it off.

We went from Newton to Betty's family's house in San Antonio for a little while. We got back home to Tampa around the middle of June. I called up Doctor Moore and Doctor Tatum and said, "Can I start practicing golf?", and they said, "Yes, by all means. You could have started in pitching and putting almost from the time you got home." So NBC television came down wanting to take some film, and I had my shorts on, and I said, "Well, I'll just go out and pitch a few."

Each day I did a bit more. The first time I played a hole at the Tampa Golf Club, I used a four iron instead of a driver, and when I finished the hole, I rode back in our little electric cart. The next day I played a hole and a half, then walked back. The day after that I went two holes.

Meanwhile George had gone out to Denver to wind up the deal on his hotel. He picked up a paper one day and saw an item, BABE ZAHARIAS PLAYS NINE HOLES. He called up all concerned. I told him, "Yeah, I went nine holes. And it felt pretty good. I shot a thirty-seven."

George was even more worried a short time later when I told him I was going to enter the Tam o' Shanter "All-American" at the end of July. But the doctors said this was all right. In fact, they told both George and Betty Dodd to encourage me on playing golf, and on getting out in public again. They said the biggest problem with colostomy patients was to get them back into normal living. They're sometimes too self-conscious about their changed condition to want to go anywhere or do anything.

216

Well, a colostomy is a big change, but the body can adjust to it. It's a wonderful thing the way the human body will correct itself if you give it a chance.

Anyway, on July thirty-first, about three-and-a-half months after the operation, I put myself to the test at the Tam o' Shanter Country Club in Niles, Illinois. They had promised in advance to pair Betty Dodd with me. She was familiar with my condition, and could step in and help if I had any trouble.

I got up there on the first tee with a big crowd of people watching me. The question in everybody's mind, and in my mind too, was, "Is Babe still capable of tournament golf?" To me, shooting tournament golf doesn't just mean getting a respectable score and finishing up among the leaders. It means being able to win. That's the standard the public has come to judge me by. It's the standard I set for myself. I wouldn't want it to be any other way.

Well, I hit that opening drive, and it sailed 250 yards straight down the middle. Those people screamed as if it was a football game. But that was about the end of my good golf for a while. I could still bang out some long ones, but I didn't seem to have the control and the touch that you need, especially on the short game.

I told you back at the start of this book how at the sixth tee in the third round, I got so discouraged that I had a little emotional breakdown. Then I finally began to pull my game together. I finished that round with a seventy-eight, after an eighty-two and an eighty-five the two previous days.

On the fourth day I shot an eighty. But some of the contestants got rained out, and they decided to wash out the whole day, and have everybody start the round over again the next day. So I went out there for the fifth day in a row to shoot eighteen holes, and this time I had an eighty-four. I wound up down in fifteenth place in the "All-American."

Only two days later I came back and played in the second Tam o' Shanter tournament, the "World Championship," and after three-and-a-half rounds I was ahead. Then I ran out of gas and took forty-three strokes to get around the last nine holes. My back was killing me, and it was an effort to swing the club. I sat down between shots and everything to rest, but it was no use. Patty Berg picked up seven strokes on the back nine to win the tournament with a 300 score. Louise Suggs was second with 303. I wound up third with 304.

It was disappointing to lose out at the end, and yet I was encouraged that I could stay up there as long as I did that soon after the operation. My performance brought me a great many inspiring letters. Those letters sort of built up my determination to continue in golf. It meant a lot to know that so many people were rooting for me in my comeback.

The only other tournament I entered in 1953 was the Texas Women's Open in October. Betsy Rawls put me out in the quarterfinals. Incidentally, in spite of having the cancer operation and missing a lot of tournaments that year, I still wound up No. 6 on the list of money-winners in women's golf for 1953, with a total of $6345 in prize money.

In January of 1954 I was back on the tour. I started out by placing seventh in the Tampa Women's Open. Then at St. Petersburg I tied for first place with Beverly Hanson. We had a sudden-death playoff, and she outlasted me. She won it on the third extra hole.

So the tour moved to Miami Beach on February eighteenth for the Serbin Women's Open. At this point ten months had gone by since my operation. People were beginning to ask each other whether I'd ever be capable of winning tournaments again. And I was asking myself the same thing.

CHAPTER 18

In the Serbin Women's Open tournament in February of 1954, I found myself battling for first place right down to the wire with Patty Berg. We both were two strokes under women's par for the first three rounds with scores of 220. On the outgoing nine holes the last day, we both hit par on the nose.

I began tiring again on the back nine, but for every hole where I slipped over par, there was another where I made it up with a birdie. I came up to the last tee still even with par for that day—and needing one more par to beat out Patty Berg.

The last hole was a long one—a par five. And I hit my

drive way over in the palm trees. I was in a real tough spot. There were palm leaves hanging down almost to the ground in front of me, and then there was a trap beyond them. I saw that I'd have to hit the ball right into those palm leaves if I was going to carry over the trap and get some distance.

I took a four-iron and swung, and that shot came off exactly as I planned. It busted a hole right through the palm leaves and carried to within a nine-iron of the green. It landed on a sandy part of the fairway. Then I played a three-quarter shot with my nine-iron—I've never studied a shot more carefully—and blasted the ball onto the green. I got down in two putts all right to make my par and win my first tournament since the cancer operation. And that was just about my biggest thrill in sports.

It was around this time that I got to go to the White House and see President and Mrs. Eisenhower. They're such nice people. I went up there for a ceremony to open the annual Cancer Crusade. There was a connection rigged up from the White House to Times Square in New York. We were to press a button in the White House and it would light up a big electric sign in Times Square.

I was presented to Mrs. Eisenhower, and I said, "Mrs. Eisenhower, I've fixed up my bangs tonight so I can be right in unison with you."

She said, "Oh, but your bangs look so nicely curled, and mine never do."

When Ike was about to enter the room, they announced, "Mr. President!" We all stood at attention while he came in.

He shook hands with me, and I said, "How do you do, Mr. President."

He said, "How do you do, Mrs. Zaharias." Then he

dropped his head and pretended to whisper. "I'll see you later, Babe," he said. "I want to talk to you about this game of golf."

And we did talk golf after the picture-taking and everything was over. I've heard, and I can believe, that he could be a real fine golfer if he had more time for it. He said we'd have to have a game together, and I hope things will work out so I can play golf with Ike some day.

I went on to have a pretty good tournament year in 1954 after winning that Serbin Women's Open in February. From there on I was in the first three just about every time out. A real high spot for me was the National Women's Open, which I'd missed playing in for two straight years on account of my operations.

I'd won the National Capital Women's Open in Washington on May sixteenth, and I didn't enter any more tournaments after that until the Open, which was being held on June thirtieth at the Salem Country Club in Peabody, Massachusetts. That's a real golf course—6393 yards long, with a men's par of seventy-two.

For a while before that tournament George and Betty Dodd and I visited at the home of one of my best golfing friends, Mrs. Peggy Kirk Bell. Peggy and her husband live in Findlay, Ohio. I was out playing golf every day and getting myself in good shape.

George and I left ahead of the others and drove up to the Salem Country Club a few days before the start of the Open. I practiced the course about three days in a row, and then rested the last day. The schedule called for eighteen holes on Thursday and eighteen on Friday, then thirty-six holes on Saturday. Having to play those two final rounds in a single day was my only worry.

The length of the course turned out to be too much for a majority of the girls. Most of them couldn't come close to the men's par of seventy-two. I jumped right into the lead with a seventy-two the first day, and I widened it in every round after that. My second-round score was seventy-one. I had a seventy-three the last morning. In the afternoon fatigue finally began to set in. I was under par for thirteen holes, then I had only one par the rest of the way. But I still shot seventy-five for the round and 291 for the tournament. Betty Hicks in second place was twelve strokes back.

It's a funny thing, but as tired as I was playing out that last round, I didn't feel tired at all once I came off the course and got in the shower. I was too happy and thrilled over the way I'd come back to win the biggest title in women's golf.

All during that 1954 National Women's Open the reporters did everything they could to make things easy for me. Instead of trying to get separate stories from me, they all got together at the end of the day and had me come in for a press conference, and after ten or fifteen minutes of questions I was through.

The reporters and photographers always have been about the best friends I've got. Some athletes complain about the press. Not me. When those boys want a story, I know they're working on a job, and if I can make their job easier for them, I'm going to do it. If it's a nice story, and a clean story, then I'm going to help them all I can.

The sportswriters who participate in the annual Associated Press polls voted me the No. 1 woman athlete for the sixth time in 1954. In addition to winning the National Women's Open by twelve strokes, I also won the Tam o' Shanter "All-American" a month later by eight strokes with a score of 294. That was only one stroke above my own seventy-two-hole women's record for the course.

I tried for the Tam o' Shanter "World Championship" too, but I was fourth in that with 304. Louise Suggs won it with 298. Those two tournaments together just got me. That was my one problem in golf after the cancer operation. I didn't have quite as much stamina as I used to. I couldn't always stay strong through four full rounds, especially if I tried to keep going in tournament after tournament.

After the "World" I went over to a tournament in Wichita, Kansas, and didn't play well. Next I competed in Ardmore, Oklahoma. I didn't play well there either, but there was one nice thing that I remember. They gave me a palomino horse named Superman. I rode him up on the eighteenth green at the presentation. That old horse just pranced up there. They announced on the microphone, "Here comes Superman, ridden by Superwoman!" I have him down at the Fort Worth Horse Shoe Club today.

I sort of petered out in the last part of 1954. Still, I won a total of $14,452 in prize money, which left me second on the list for the year.

All the while I was doing a lot of things besides competing for golf prizes. That goes back to a promise I made in my prayers when I was in the hospital waiting for my cancer operation. I promised God that if He made me well, I'd do everything in my power when I got out to help the fight against cancer.

And when I did get out, I remembered that promise and

224

said yes to everything I went out to Seattle to open a Babe Didrikson Zaharias chapter of the American Cancer Society. I kept making trips for personal appearances, and did radio and television spots for the American Cancer Society and the Damon Runyon Foundation. Wherever I went for a tournament, I generally did some cancer work there. A priest or somebody would ask me to visit cancer patients he knew, and try to raise their spirits, and I was glad to do it.

But toward the end of 1954 I had to halfway break my promise to God and cut down on my cancer work some, because it was wearing me down, along with all the other things I had to do. And I've gotten to when I like to spend more time at home. Housework has always been a treat to me, which is why I've never had a full-time maid. I've spent so much of my life away on the road that when I get home I'm just aching to put my hands in the dishwasher, and make up the beds, and vacuum the carpets.

Until 1955 we lived in a nice little converted caddy house right on the grounds of our Tampa Golf & Country Club. We sold the club in 1954, but the new owner said to take our time moving out. We finally built a new home of our own, and moved into it in March of 1955. It's only a short distance from the other house, on a pond at the edge of the golf course.

We sort of splurged on that house, but we think it's worth it. We spent what it cost to get everything we wanted. I'd been dreaming of building a home since I was a little girl. And traveling around the way I have all these years, and visiting different people, I had a lot of ideas stored up about what I'd like in my "dream house." I'd never really had a chance to try my ideas out. At the other places we've lived in—Los Angeles, Denver, Sky Crest—we took houses that were already built.

Once George gave the go-ahead on our new Tampa home, I got busy with the plans. I'd take along books on home decoration on my trips. I had my pad and ruler and pencil, and I started getting my design ideas down on paper. During one plane ride I did the kitchen, with the dinette set off by wrought-iron work and everything. On another trip I mapped out the patio. The master bathroom was my design, with its two wash stands, and the master bedroom, with its louvred doors. And I marked in all the windows, and the types I wanted. I designed just about everything in the house. The architects would take my drawings and work out the final blueprints.

I watched that house go up all through the different stages of building. Sometimes I'd get in there and drive nails with the carpenters. I did some of the mortar work out on the patio. I worked with the electricians and all.

I planned everything big and roomy, for George's comfort. He's a big man. George has had a physical problem too. In 1954 he developed a diabetic condition. For a time he had to take insulin. He got off that after a while, but ever since, he's had to regulate his diet very carefully.

You couldn't call our new place one certain type of house. It's a blend of different things. It's one story, which sounds like a ranch house, but it's really more of a traditional house. The bedrooms are colonial and Early American, with a little Pennsylvania Dutch at the windows. The living room is a country-squire drawing room. The kitchen is sort of California ranch, with a mixture of Arizona ranch.

As for golf, the Tampa Golf & Country Club course is

practically our back yard. Most of the girls on the tournament circuit go out and play golf just about every day. I always used to do that myself, but what with one thing and another, I haven't been able to practice too regularly the past few years.

I've been experimenting a little bit, though. I've realized that I am getting older, and that the time was coming for me to change over from a bashing type of game to a smoother type of game. When you begin to lose some of your power, then you have to develop more finesse. You have to change your style a little.

I've sometimes thought that my biggest trouble in golf was knowing so many different ways to play shots. I mean, I can hit low shots or fade shots or push shots or slices or hooks or whatever I want. At times I've felt that I might be better off if I knew just one way to hit the ball, and always played it straightaway.

It's hard to keep your golf game in the groove if you aren't getting steady practice. And then there's another way in which too many distractions can reduce your effectiveness as a tournament player. I'm talking about the mental side of the game—the mental concentration you need for big-time competition.

Here's what I mean. When I'm playing in a tournament, and I'm feeling sharp and rested, then every time I get set to play a shot, I can see a certain spot out there where I want to hit the ball. I know what part of the fairway I want to reach to give myself an easy approach to the green, and that sort of thing.

But when I've been thinking about too many other things besides golf, and my mind isn't clear and easy out there, then

227

I don't plan my shots the way you should. I don't see the one right place where the ball should go. I'm not alert to the different possibilities of the situation. I'm just keeping the ball in play.

You won't often win anything when your mind is in that state. But then, winning doesn't always seem as important to me now as it did when I was younger. I guess I've mellowed down. It used to just kill me to get beat. I wanted to win everything I played. But I've been at the top in sports for a quarter of a century, starting with when I first made the women's All-American basketball team as a young kid in 1930. And I've been putting my golf shoes on and taking them off for a long time. You can get a little tired of that. At times I feel I'd rather just ride around the course in my electric cart, or sit on the clubhouse porch, and let the rest of the girls fight it out.

People would say to me when I came back to the tournament circuit after my cancer operation, "Why don't you just take life easy?" My doctors would tell me not to drive myself so hard. George would say, "You've proved everything. You don't have to prove anything more."

There are several reasons why I didn't retire from golf after that 1953 cancer business—and still don't intend to retire, in spite of my 1955 ailments. One reason is that every time I get out and play well in a golf tournament, it seems to buck up people with the same cancer trouble I had. I can tell that from the letters I keep getting. I just wish I could find the time to acknowledge all those letters personally. With the ones from colostomy patients, I've tried at least to send them a form I've made up that answers the most important questions about colostomies. It's a widespread problem—there are something like 10,000 colostomy operations performed every year, according to the American Cancer Society.

Another reason why I've kept coming back to the golf circuit is that I helped start the Ladies' Professional Golf Association, and I want to help it keep on growing. The Ladies' PGA has been building up right along in tournaments and purses and good players. At first there were just six or seven of us. Now we've got about twenty-five or thirty girls who are very fine golfers. I know the tournaments draw better when all of us are in there than when some of us aren't.

Finally, there's this. Since I began having my medical troubles, any time I've played two or three tournaments in a row without winning, people have started saying, "What's the matter with Babe? Is she through?" And then I get back to where I don't want to get beat. I get that old desire to win. I want to go out and prove all over again that I'm still a championship golfer.

This sometimes leads to my overdoing things. It was like that on the winter tour in 1955. I started off by winning the Tampa Women's Open in January, although I was tiring at the end. I lost four strokes to par on the last five holes, and just did hang on to first place with a 298 total, one stroke ahead of Louise Suggs.

Then I didn't win my next couple of tournaments. At Sarasota in February I didn't even finish. I shot a seventy-nine the first day on that little old course. I just couldn't make myself play golf. I had a virus. I was taking penicillin and aureomycin.

I said to George, "Instead of letting myself down, and letting the public down, by trying to play when I can't play,

I'm going to get out of here." So I withdrew after that first round. And the reporters were buzzing around George, wondering whether I was seriously sick.

I went home to Tampa to rest up, but what with our new house being in the final stages, and with trying to keep up my side activities, I didn't rest as well as I should have. I came back for the Titleholders tournament at Augusta in the middle of March, and didn't play too well in that. At the finish I was tied for sixth place.

My second-year cancer check-up was due in Beaumont on April eleventh. I was feeling so draggy that I decided to have a general check-up before the cancer one. The doctor said I was rundown, and on the anemic side. He told me I should take a real vacation.

So I went with Betty Dodd and her sister Peggy to a cabin on the Gulf coast of Texas. This was around the end of March. We fished and loafed and had a wonderful time. But there was one unlucky thing that happened. One day we got our car stuck in the sand. The three of us jacked it up and got it out of there. We started up the car—and went right back in the sand. So we had to get it out all over again.

Well, with the strain of all that lifting and tugging, I apparently did something to my back. It was bothering me some, but when I went through my cancer check in Beaumont and they found no signs of any recurrence, the back didn't worry me any more. I was all pepped up again. I jumped right back on the tournament circuit, which I know now was a mistake.

I went into the Babe Zaharias Open at Beaumont on April fifteenth and faded off to thirteenth place with a terrible eighty on the last day. My back was aching and everything.

230

I thought it was just fatigue. Instead of laying off for a while, I went on to Georgia the next week for the Carrollton Women's Open. I took vitamin B-1 injections during the tournament to try and keep up my strength, but the best I could do was tie for sixth.

I still wasn't ready to admit that I wasn't in condition to play. I was more determined than ever to win one. I moved up with the tour the next week to Spartanburg, South Carolina, to play in the Peach Blossom-Betsy Rawls tournament. And I did win. I shot a seventy-two, then a seventy, then a seventy-five and finally a seventy-six. My 293 total put me in first place by two strokes over Marilyn Smith.

That tournament was an ordeal for me toward the end. My back was really hurting. I came home to Tampa and practically collapsed. I was in bed for several days. I figured some rest was all I needed. Each week I kept expecting to get back on the circuit. But I was having pains in my right leg and numbness in my right foot.

My condition got worse instead of better. Finally I went down to Galveston in late May to the John Sealy Hospital to see Doctor Robert Moore, the man who did my 1953 cancer operation. He called in some of the other specialists there for consultation, and my back trouble was diagnosed as a slipped disc.

They had me try therapy and special exercises for a while. The back didn't respond. Then they put me in traction. That didn't work either. I was in almost constant agony by now. After nearly two weeks in traction, I was operated on for a ruptured disc of the spinal column by Doctor S. R. Snodgrass at the John Sealy Hospital.

That was on June 22, 1955. For a while afterward I was

convalescing nicely in the hospital, and then I began having new pains in my back. At the end of July I got some bad news. They spotted a trace of new cancer on the right side of my sacrum, which is at the rear part of the pelvis.

So x-ray treatments were started. The doctors said it would be three to six months before I could get back to the golf tournaments. And just as in 1953, a lot of people were doubting that I ever would get back in competition.

As far as I was concerned, there was no doubt about my coming back again. With the love and support of the many friends I have made, how could I miss? They have helped me hurdle one obstacle after another, and any success I have had is due to a great extent to their devotion and consideration. Right now I want to thank them one and all, as well as the many unknown people who have befriended me and helped me on my way. Winning has always meant much to me, but winning friends has meant the most.

In the future, maybe I'll have to limit myself to just a few of the most important tournaments each year. But I expect to be shooting for championships for a good many years to come. My autobiography isn't finished yet.

September 1955

Index

236

Babe Zaharias' Record

1932 . .Voted Woman Athlete of the Year by Associated Press.

1935. .Began playing golf.

1940. .Winner, Western Open, 5 & 4. Winner, Texas Open, 1 up.

1944. .Winner and Medalist, 77, Western Open, 7 & 5.

1945. .Winner and Medalist, 75, Western Open, 4 & 2. Winner, Texas Open, 7 & 6. Runner-up, Western Amateur. Voted Woman Athlete of the Year by Associated Press.

1946. .Winner and Medalist, 73, Trans-Mississippi Championship, 6 & 5. Winner, National Amateur, 10 & 9. Winner, All American Open, 310. Winner, Texas Open, 5 & 3. Winner, Broadmoor Inv., 6 & 4. Voted Woman Athlete of the Year by Associated Press.

1947. .Winner, Tampa (Fla.) Open, 306. Winner, Helen Doherty, 12 & 10. Winner, Palm Beach, 1 up. Winner, South Atlantic, 5 & 4. Winner, Florida East Coast, 2 & 1. Winner, Augusta Titleholders, 304. Winner, North and South, 5 & 4. Winner, British Amateur, 5 & 4. Winner, Hollywood, Fla. Four-Ball.

Winner, Florida Mixed Two-Ball.
Winner and Medalist, 148, Celebrities Championship, Wash. D. C.
Winner, Broadmoor Inv., 10 & 9.
Voted Woman Athlete of the Year by Associated Press.

1948. .Tied second, Augusta Title-holders Tournament, 309. Winner, All American Tournament, 309—$1,200. Winner, World Championship, 149—$1,000. Winner, National Open, 300—$1,200. Runner-up, Texas Open. Runner-up, Western Open. Runner-up, Hardscrabble Open.

1949. .Runner-up, Tampa (Fla.) Open, 296—$650. Second Pro, Augusta Title-holders Tournament, 304 Winner, Eastern Open, 219—$1,000. Quarter-finalist, Western Open. Winner, World Championship, 301—$1,000. Runner-up, All American Tournament, 307—$650. Runner-up, National Open, 305—$1,000. Semi-finalist, Hardscrabble Open. Voted Greatest Female Athlete of half century by Associated Press.

1950. .Third Pro, Tampa Open, 304 —$650.

240

1950 (*continued*)

Winner, Augusta Titleholders Tournament, 298—$700.

Winner, 144 Hole Weathervane Tournament, 629—$7,450.

Runner-up, Eastern Open, 218.

Winner, Western Open, $500.

Winner, All American Championship, 296—$900.

Winner, World Championship, 298—$2,000.

Winner, National Open, 291—$1,250.

Voted Woman Athlete of the Year by Associated Press.

1951..Winner, Ponte Vedra (Fla.) Open, 223—$750.

Winner, Tampa Open, 288—$1,000. Set 72-hole record.

Winner, Orlando Two-Ball Tournament, with George Bolesta.

Tied Second Pro, Augusta Titleholders Tournament, 312—$325.

Runner-up, Sandhills Open, 231—$500.

Winner, Fresno Open, 225—$750.

Winner, Richmond Open, 224—$750.

Tied second, Sacramento Open, 76—$137 50.

Runner-up, 144 hole Weathervane, 601. Lost to Patty Berg, 36-hole play-off, 146-147—$2,500

Runner-up, Eastern Open, 218—$600.

Winner, All American Tournament, 295—$1,000.

Winner, World Championship, 298—$2,100

Runner-up, Carrollton Open, 222—$500.

Third, National Open, 299—$900.

Winner, Texas Open, 8 & 7.

Leading money winner—$15,087.50.

1952..Tied third, Jacksonville Open, 236—$275.

Runner-up, Tampa Open, 298—$750.

Winner, Miami Weathervane, 145—$750.

Winner, Orlando Two-Ball with Al Besselink, 1 up—$500.

Tied second, Sarasota Open, 73.

Winner Augusta Titleholders, 299—$1,000.

Tied fifth, New Orleans Open, 311—$350.

Runner-up, Houston Weathervane, 143—$540.

Fifth, Richmond Open, 225—$270

Winner, Fresno Open, 226—$1,175.

Third, World Championship, 308—$1,000.

Tied sixth, Betty Jameson Open, 222—$285.

Winner, Texas Open, 7 & 6—$300.

Fifth Money Winner—$7,503.25.

1953..Sixth, Tampa Open, 300—$450.

Tied second, Miami Beach Open, 222—$560.

Runner-up, Orlando Two-Ball teamed with George Bolesta—$458.34.

Winner, Sarasota Open, 217—$875.

Tied second, Jacksonville Open, 216—$560.

Tied second, New Orleans Open, 231—$630.

Winner, Babe Zaharias Open, 217—$875.

Tied 15th, All American Open, 329.

Third, World Championship, 307—$1,000.

Awarded Ben Hogan Trophy for Greatest Comeback of the Year.

Sixth Money Winner—$6,345.42.

1954..Tied 14th, Sea Island Open,
246.
Seventh, Tampa Open, 316—
$425.
Runner-up, St. Petersburg,
216—lost play-off—$630.
Winner, Serbin Open, 294—
$1,200.
Winner, Sarasota Open, 223—
$875.
Third, Augusta Titleholders,
302—$400
Third, Betsy Rawls Open, 221
—$490.
Third, Carrollton Open, 220—
$490.
Third, New Orleans Open, 299
—$660.
Runner-up, Babe Zaharias
Open, 226—$500.
Winner, National Capital
Open, 299—$1,000.
Winner, National Open, 291—
$2,000.
Tied second, Inverness Four-
Ball, 141—$475.

Fifth, Fort Wayne Open, 223
—$287.
Winner, All American Open,
294—$1,000.
Fourth, World Championship,
304—$800.
Fourth, Wichita Open, 305—
$500
Tied seventh, Ardmore Open,
312—$780
Second money winner—
$14,452.
Winner Vare Trophy Av.
Score 75 48.

1955..Fourth, Los Angeles Open,
226—$500.
Winner, Tampa Open, 298—
$1,000.
Fourth, St Petersburg Open,
302—$500.
Winner, Serbin Diamond Golf
Ball.
Ninth, Serbin Open, 310—
$200.
Tied seventh, Augusta Title-
holders, 306—$280.

CPSIA information can be obtained
at www.ICGtesting.com
Printed in the USA
LVHW011247290620
659286LV00011B/1684

9 780343 291440